U.S. Fish and Wildlife Service

Waterfowl

Population Status, 2006

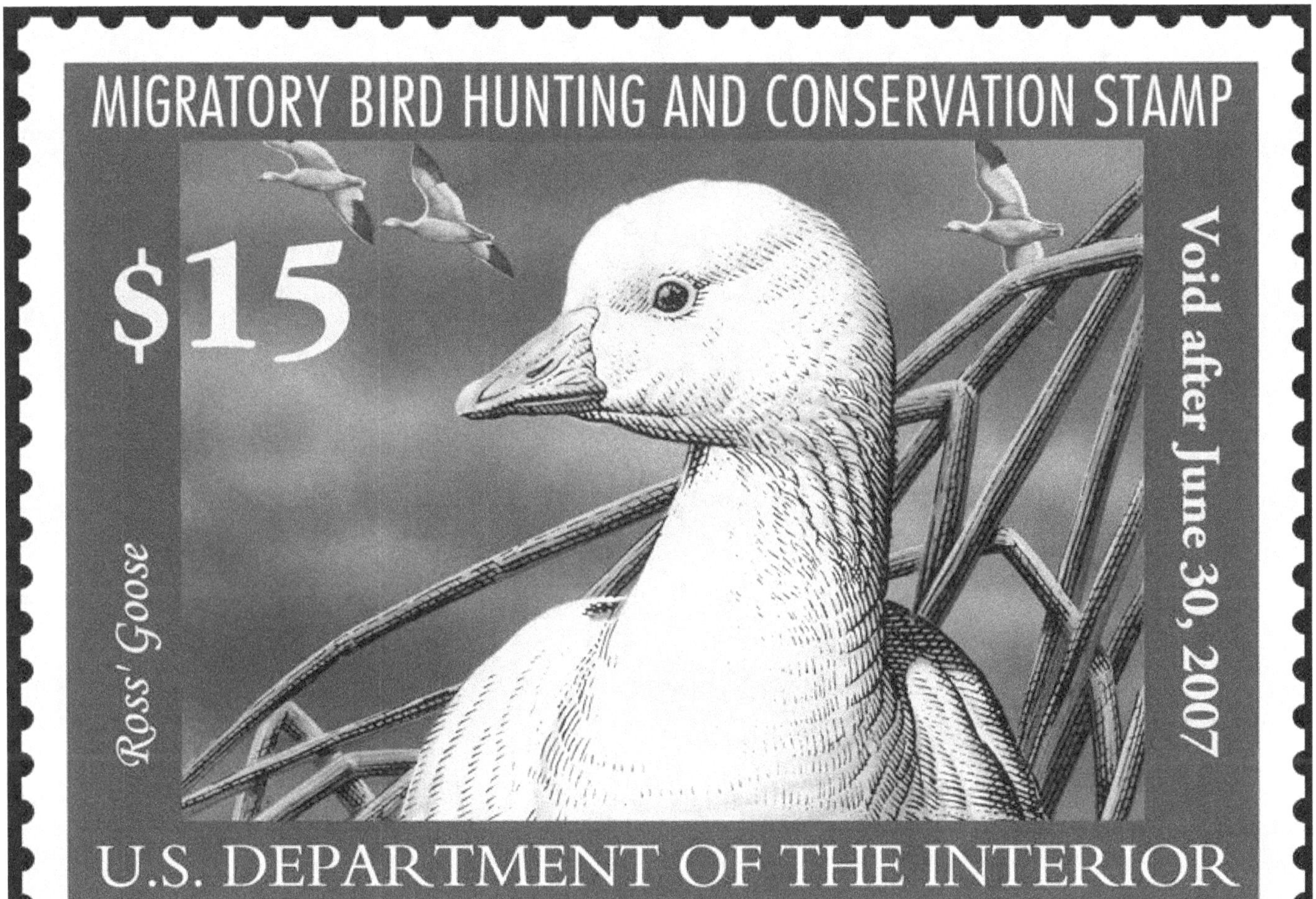
MIGRATORY BIRD HUNTING AND CONSERVATION STAMP
$15
Void after June 30, 2007
Ross' Goose
U.S. DEPARTMENT OF THE INTERIOR

WATERFOWL POPULATION STATUS, 2006

July 25, 2006

In North America the process of establishing hunting regulations for waterfowl is conducted annually. In the United States the process involves a number of scheduled meetings in which information regarding the status of waterfowl is presented to individuals within the agencies responsible for setting hunting regulations. In addition the proposed regulations are published in the *Federal Register* to allow public comment. This report includes the most current breeding population and production information available for waterfowl in North America and is a result of cooperative efforts by the U.S. Fish and Wildlife Service (FWS), the Canadian Wildlife Service (CWS), various state and provincial conservation agencies, and private conservation organizations. This report is intended to aid the development of waterfowl harvest regulations in the United States for the 2006-2007 hunting season.

ACKNOWLEDGMENTS

Waterfowl Population and Habitat Information: The information contained in this report is the result of the efforts of numerous individuals and organizations. Principal contributors include the Canadian Wildlife Service, U.S. Fish and Wildlife Service, state wildlife conservation agencies, provincial conservation agencies from Canada, and Direccion General de Conservacion Ecologica de los Recursos Naturales, Mexico. In addition, several conservation organizations, other state and federal agencies, universities, and private individuals provided information or cooperated in survey activities. Some habitat and weather information was taken from the NOAA/USDA Joint Agriculture Weather Facility (http://www.cpc.ncep.noaa.gov/index.html), Environment Canada (http://www.pnr-rpn.ec.gc.ca/index.en.html), and Waterfowl Population Surveys reports (http://migratorybirds.fws.gov/reports/reports.html). Appendix A provides a list of individuals responsible for the collection and compilation of data for the Ducks section of this report. Appendix B provides a list of individuals who were primary contacts for information included in the Geese and Swans section. We apologize for any omission of individuals from these lists, and thank all participants for their contributions. Without this combined effort, a comprehensive assessment of waterfowl populations and habitat would not be possible.

Authors: This report was prepared by the U.S. Fish and Wildlife Service, Division of Migratory Bird Management, Branch of Surveys and Assessment. The principal authors are Pamela R. Garrettson, Timothy J. Moser, and Khristi Wilkins. The authors compiled information from the numerous sources to provide an assessment of the status of waterfowl populations.

Report Preparation: The preparation of this report involved substantial efforts on the part of many individuals. Support for the processing of data and publication was provided by Mark C. Otto and John Sauer. Ray Bentley, John Bidwell, Karen Bollinger, Elizabeth Huggins, Bruce Conant, Carl Ferguson, Rod King, Mark Koneff, Fred Roetker, John Solberg, Phil Thorpe, Dan Nieman, Dale Caswell, James Dubovsky, Robert Blohm, and James Wortham provided habitat narratives, reviewed portions of the report that addressed major breeding areas, and provided helpful comments.

This report should be cited as: U.S. Fish and Wildlife Service. 2006. Waterfowl population status, 2006. U.S. Department of the Interior, Washington, D.C. U.S.A.

All Division of Migratory Bird Management reports are available at our home page (http://www.fws.gov/migratorybirds).

Table of Contents

ACKNOWLEDGMENTS..2

Status of Ducks

METHODS 5
RESULTS AND DISCUSSION...7
REFERENCES...30

Status of Geese and Swans

METHODS 31
RESULTS AND DISCUSSION...33

Appendices

Appendix A. Individuals who supplied information on the status of ducks 47
Appendix B. Individuals who supplied information on the status of geese and swans....................49
Appendix C. Strata and transects of the Waterfowl Breeding Population and Habitat Survey.........51
Appendix D. Estimated number of May ponds and standard errors in portions of Prairie and
            Parkland Canada and the northcentral U.S. 52
Appendix E. Breeding population estimates for total ducks and mallards for states, provinces,
            or regions that conduct spring surveys 53
Appendix F. Breeding population estimates and standard errors for 10 species of ducks
            from the traditional survey area 55
Appendix G. Total breeding duck estimates for the traditional survey area, in
            thousands...57
Appendix H. Breeding population estimates and 95% confidence intervals or credibility intervals
            for the 10 most abundant species of ducks in the eastern survey area.........................58
Appendix I. Population indices for North American Canada goose populations, 1969-2005 59
Appendix J. Population indices for light goose, greater white-fronted goose, brant, emperor
            goose, and tundra swan populations during 1969-2005 60

List of Duck Tables

Table 1. Estimated number of May ponds in portions of Prairie and Parkland Canada and the northcentral U.S. 9
Table 2. Total duck breeding population estimates 12
Table 3. Mallard breeding population estimates 13
Table 4. Gadwall breeding population estimates 19
Table 5. American wigeon breeding population estimates 19
Table 6. Green-winged teal breeding population estimates 20
Table 7. Blue-winged teal breeding population estimates 20
Table 8. Northern shoveler breeding population estimates 21
Table 9. Northern pintail breeding population estimates 21
Table 10. Redhead breeding population estimates 22
Table 11. Canvasback breeding population estimates 22
Table 12. Scaup (greater and lesser combined) breeding population estimates 23
Table 13. Duck breeding population estimates for the 10 most abundant species in the eastern survey area 23

List of Duck Figures

Figure 1. Number of ponds in May and 90% confidence intervals for Prairie and Parkland Canada and the northcentral U.S. 9
Figure 2. Breeding population estimates, 90% confidence intervals, and North American Waterfowl Management Plan population goal for selected species for the traditional survey area 14
Figure 3. Breeding population estimates and 95% credibility intervals for selected species in the eastern survey area 17
Figure 4. Breeding population estimates and 95% confidence intervals for selected species in the eastern survey area 18
Figure 5. Estimates and 90% confidence intervals for the size of the mallard population in the fall 30

List of Goose and Swan Figures

Figure 1. Important goose nesting areas in arctic and subarctic North America 32
Figure 2. Snow and ice cover in North America for spring 33
Figure 3. Approximate ranges of Canada goose populations in North America 34
Figures 4-18. Indices to Canada goose populations' status 33-40
Figure 19. Approximate ranges of selected goose populations in North America 41
Figures 20-27. Indices to selected goose populations' status 42-45
Figure 28. Approximate range of Emperor goose and tundra swan populations in North America 46
Figure 29. Indices to tundra swan populations' status 46

STATUS OF DUCKS

Abstract: In the Waterfowl Breeding Population and Habitat Survey traditional survey area (strata 1-18, 20-50, and 75-77), the total duck population estimate was 36.2 ± 0.6 [SE] million birds. This was 14% greater than last year's estimate of 31.7 ± 0.6 million birds and 9% above the 1955-2005 long-term average. Mallard (*Anas platyrhynchos*) abundance was 7.3 ± 0.2 million birds, which was similar to last year's estimate of 6.8 ± 0.3 million birds and to the long-term average. Blue-winged teal (*A. discors*) abundance was 5.9 ± 0.3 million birds. This value was 28% greater than last year's estimate of 4.6 ± 0.2 million birds and 30% above the long-term average. The estimated abundance of green-winged teal (*A. crecca*; 2.6 ± 0.2 million) was 20% greater than last year and 39% above the long-term average. The estimated number of gadwall (*A. strepera*; 2.8 ± 0.2 million) was 30% greater than last year and was 67% above the long-term average, and the estimated number of redheads (*Aythya americana*; 0.9 ± 0.1 million) increased 55% relative to 2005 and was 47% above the long-term average. The canvasback estimate (*A. valisineria*; 0.7 ± 0.1 million) was 33% higher than last year's and was 23% higher than the long-term average. The Northern shoveler (*Anas clypeata*; 3.7 ± 0.2 million) estimate was similar to last year's, and 69% above the long-term average. Although estimates for most species increased relative to last year and were greater than their long-term averages, American wigeon (*A. americana*; 2.2 ± 0.1 million) and scaup (*Aythya affinis* and *A. marila* combined; 3.2 ± 0.2 million) estimates were unchanged relative to 2005, but remained 17% and 37% below their long-term averages, respectively. The estimate for scaup was a record low for the second consecutive year. The Northern pintail (*Anas acuta*; 3.4 ± 0.2 million) estimate was 18% below its 1955-2005 average, although this year's estimate was 32% greater than that of last year. The total May pond estimate (Prairie Canada and U.S. combined) was 6.1 ± 0.2 million ponds. This was 13% greater than last year's estimate of 5.4 ± 0.2 million and 26% higher than the long-term average of 4.8 ± 0.1 million ponds. The 2006 estimate of ponds in Prairie Canada was 4.4 ± 0.2 million ponds, a 13% increase from last year's estimate of 3.9 ± 0.2 million ponds and 32% above the 1955-2005 average. The 2006 pond estimate for the north-central U.S. (1.6 ± 0.1 million) was similar to last year's estimate and to the long-term average. The projected mallard fall flight index was 9.8 ± 0.1 million, similar to the 2005 estimate of 9.3 ± 0.1 million birds. The eastern survey area was restratified in 2005, and is now composed of strata 51-72. Mergansers (red-breasted [*Mergus serrator*], common [*M. merganser*], and hooded [*Lophodytes cucullatus*;]), mallards, American black ducks (*A. rubripes*), Ring-necked ducks (*Aythya collaris*), goldeneyes (common [*Bucephala clangula*] and Barrow's [*B. islandica*]) and green-winged teal were all similar to their 2005 estimates. American wigeon (-51%) and buffleheads ([*B. albeola*], -58%) were lower than their 2005 estimates. None of the species in the eastern survey area differed from long-term averages.

This section summarizes the most recent information about the status of North American duck populations and their habitats in order to facilitate development of harvest regulations in the U.S. The U.S. Fish and Wildlife Service and its partners conduct a variety of surveys to collect information on ducks. The annual status of these populations is assessd using databases resulting from these surveys, which include estimates of the size of breeding populations, production, and harvest. This report details abundance estimates and production outlooks; harvest survey results are discussed in separate reports. The data and analyses were the most current available when this report was written. Future analyses may yield slightly different results as databases are updated and new analytical procedures become available.

METHODS

Breeding Population and Habitat Survey

Federal, provincial, and state agencies conduct surveys each spring to estimate the size of breeding populations and to evaluate habitat conditions. These surveys are conducted using fixed-wing aircraft and helicopters, and cover over 2.0 million square miles that encompass principal breeding areas of North America. The traditional survey area (strata 1-18, 20-50, and 75-77) comprises parts of Alaska, Canada, and the northcentral U.S., and includes approximately 1.3 million square miles (Appendix C). The eastern survey area (strata 51-72) includes parts of Ontario, Quebec, Labrador, Newfoundland, Nova Scotia, Prince Edward Island, New Brunswick, New York, and Maine, covering an area of approximately 0.7 million square miles.

In Prairie and Parkland Canada and the north-central U.S., aerial waterfowl counts are corrected annually for visibility bias by conducting ground counts. In the northern portions of the traditional survey area and the eastern survey area, duck estimates are adjusted using visibility correction factors derived from a comparison of airplane and helicopter counts. Annual estimates of duck abundance are available since 1955 for the traditional survey area and since 1996 for all strata (except 57-59, 69) in the eastern survey area. However, portions of the eastern survey area have been surveyed since 1990. In the traditional survey area, estimates of pond abundance in Prairie Canada are available since 1961 and in the northcentral U.S. since 1974. Several provinces and states also conduct breeding waterfowl surveys using various methods; some have survey designs that allow calculation of measures of precision for their estimates. Information about habitat conditions was supplied primarily by biologists working in the survey areas. However, much ancillary weather information was obtained from agricultural and weather internet sites (see references). Unless otherwise noted, z-tests were used for assessing statistical significance, with alpha levels (P-value) set at 0.1; actual P-values are given in tables along with wetland and waterfowl estimates.

Since 1990 the U.S. Fish and Wildlife Service (USFWS) has conducted aerial transect surveys using fixed-wing aircraft in eastern Canada and the northeast U.S., similar to those used in the mid-continent, for estimating waterfowl abundance. Additionally, the Canadian Wildlife Service (CWS) has conducted a helicopter-based aerial plot survey in core American black duck breeding regions of Ontario, Quebec, and the Atlantic Provinces. Historically, data from these surveys were analyzed separately, despite geographic overlap in survey coverage. In 2004, the USFWS and CWS agreed to integrate the two surveys, produce composite estimates from both sets of survey data, and expand the geographic scope of the survey in eastern North America.

As a result, as of 2005, waterfowl population estimates for eastern North America are no longer produced solely on the basis of USFWS-collected data, but are be based on both USFWS and CWS data. Estimates of populations in eastern North America (strata 51-72) are now derived as composite estimates based on data from the CWS and USFWS surveys. For strata containing both CWS and USFWS data (51, 52, 63, 64, 66, and 68), visibility-adjusted USFWS data were combined with plot data; single survey results were used as the estimates for strata containing only one source of information (53, 54, 55, 56, 57,

58, 59, 62, 65, and 69 for transects; 70, 71, and 72 for plots). In cases where the USFWS has traditionally not recorded observations to the species level (i.e., scoters [Melanitta spp.], mergansers, goldeneyes), only CWS plot survey data were used in estimation. While estimates were generated for all strata in the eastern survey area, survey-wide composite estimates for this region (Table 13) currently correspond only to strata 51, 52, 63, 64, 66, 67, 68, 70, 71, and 72. These strata are coincident with the geographic extent of the CWS helicopter plot survey. In future reports, survey-wide composite estimates will be derived for the entire region encompassed by the USFWS and CWS surveys (strata 51-72).

For widely-distributed species, (American black ducks, mallards, green-winged teal, and ring-necked duck), composite estimates of population size were constructed using a hierarchical model, in which change is modeled using a log-linear model that includes survey and transect/plot effects (e.g., Link and Sauer 2002). Area-weighted, exponentiated year effects were calculated using the log-linear model for each survey, then averaged between surveys to provide estimates of total indicated birds in each stratum. For all other species, which occur at lower densities and are more patchily distributed in the eastern survey area, this modeling approach was not suitable, and estimates for these species represent averages of visibility-adjusted FWS and CWS survey results.

To produce a consistent index for American black ducks, total indicated birds were calculated using the CWS method of scaling observed pairs. Observed black duck pairs were scaled by 1.5 rather than the 1.0 scaling traditionally applied by the USFWS. The CWS scaling is based on sex-specific observations collected during the CWS survey in eastern Canada which indicate that approximately 50% of black duck pair observations are actually 2 drakes. For other species, the standard USFWS definition of total indicated birds was used.

Changes in indices, procedures, geographic stratification, and in the area sampled by composite surveys, result in changes in the estimated population totals; therefore, survey results for eastern North America presented in this report are not directly comparable to results presented in previous reports. We anticipate additional refinements to the survey design and analysis for eastern North America during the coming years, and composite estimates are subject to change in the future.

Production and Habitat Survey

For the past three years, we have had no traditional July Production and Habitat Survey to verify the early predictions of our biologists in the field, due to severe budget constraints within the migratory bird program. However, the pilot-biologists responsible for several survey areas (southern Alberta, southern Saskatchewan, the Dakotas, and Montana) returned in early July for a brief flight over representative portions of their survey areas as a rough assessment of habitat changes since May and resultant duck production. This information, along with reports from local biologists in the field, helped formulate an overall perspective on duck production this year.

Total Duck Species Composition

In the traditional survey area, our estimate of total ducks excludes scoters, eiders (*Somateria* and *Polysticta* spp.), long-tailed ducks (*Clangula hyemalis*), mergansers, and wood ducks (*Aix sponsa*), because the traditional survey area does not include a large portion of their breeding range.

Mallard Fall-flight Index

The mallard fall-flight index is a prediction of the size of the fall abundance of mallards originating from the mid-continent region of North America. For management purposes, the mid-continent population is composed of mallards originating from the traditional survey area, as well as Michigan, Minnesota, and Wisconsin. The index is based on the mallard models used for Adaptive Harvest Management, and considers breeding population size, habitat conditions, adult summer survival, and projected fall age ratio (young/adult). The projected fall age ratio is predicted from a model that depicts how the age ratio varies with changes in spring population size and pond abundance. The fall-flight index represents a weighted average of the fall flights predicted by the four alternative models of mallard population dynamics used in Adaptive Harvest Management (U. S. Fish and Wildlife Service 2006).

RESULTS AND DISCUSSION

2005 in Review

Habitat conditions at the time of the survey in May 2005 were variable, with some areas improved relative to 2004 and others that remained or became increasingly dry. The total May pond estimate (Prairie and Parkland Canada and the northcentral U.S. combined) was 5.4 ± 0.2 million ponds, which was 37% greater than the 2004 estimate of 3.9 ± 0.2 million ponds, and 12% higher than the long-term average of 4.8 ± 0.1 million ponds. Habitat in the surveyed portion of the U.S. prairies was in fair to poor condition due to a dry fall, winter, and early spring and warm winter temperatures. Nesting habitat was particularly poor in South Dakota because below-average precipitation resulted in degraded wetland conditions and increased tilling and grazing of wetland margins. Birds likely over-flew the state for wetter conditions further north. Water levels, wetland conditions, and upland nesting cover in North Dakota and eastern Montana improved markedly during June, following the survey, with the onset of well-above average precipitation.

The 2005 pond estimate for north-central U.S. (1.5 ± 0.1 million) was similar to the 2004 estimate. The prairies of southern Alberta and southwestern Saskatchewan were also quite dry in early May of 2005. The U.S. and Canadian prairies received substantial rain in late May and during the entire month of June that recharged wetlands and encouraged growth of vegetation. While this improved habitat quality on the Prairies, it came too late to benefit early-nesting species, but likely did benefit late nesting species and renesting efforts. Record high rains flooded the lower elevation prairie areas of central Manitoba during April 2005, which produced fair or poor nesting conditions for breeding waterfowl. In contrast, the Canadian Parklands were much improved relative to 2004, due to several years of improving nesting cover and above-normal precipitation the previous fall and winter. These areas were in good-to-excellent condition at the start of the survey and remained so into July. Overall, the May pond estimate in Prairie and Parkland Canada was 3.9 ± 0.2 million in 2005, which was a 56% increase over the 2004 estimate of 2.5 ± 0.1 million ponds and 17% higher than the long-term average of 3.3 ± 0.3 million ponds.

Portions of Northern Manitoba and Northern Saskatchewan also experienced flooding during 2005, which resulted in only fair conditions for breeding waterfowl. In contrast, most of the Northwest Territories was in good condition due to adequate water and a timely spring break up that made habitat available to early-nesting species. However, dry conditions in eastern parts of the Northwest Territories and northern Alberta resulted in low water levels in lakes and ponds and the complete drying of some wetlands. Therefore, habitat was also classified as fair in these areas. For the most part, habitats in Alaska were in excellent condition, with an early spring and good water levels, except for a few flooded river areas and on the North Slope, where spring was late.

In the Eastern Survey area (strata 51-72), habitat conditions were generally good during 2005 due to adequate water and relatively mild spring temperatures. Exceptions were the coast of Maine and the Atlantic Provinces, where May temperatures were cool and some flooding occurred along the coast and major rivers. Also, below-normal precipitation left some habitat in fair to poor condition in southern Ontario. However, precipitation in southern Ontario after survey completion improved habitat conditions in that region.

In the traditional survey area, the 2005 total duck population estimate (excluding scoters, eiders, long-tailed ducks, mergansers, and wood ducks) was 31.7 ± 0.6 million birds, similar to the 2004 estimate of 32.2 ± 0.6 million birds, and 5% below the long-term (1955-2004) average. In the eastern Dakotas, total duck numbers were 14% below their 2004 estimate, but remained 10% above the long-term average. Counts in southern Alberta were 27% higher than the previous year's, but remained 26% below the long-term average. The total-duck estimate increased 38% relative to 2004 in southern Saskatchewan and was 9% above the long-term average. Total duck estimates in central and northern Alberta, northeastern British Columbia and the Northwest Territories were 20% below the 2004 estimate and 35% below the long-term average. Counts in the northern Saskatchewan—northern Manitoba--western Ontario area, and the western Dakotas--Eastern Montana survey areas were 21% and 20% below 2004 estimates, respectively, and 10% and 20% below their long-term averages. In the Alaska--Yukon Territory--Old Crow Flats region the total duck estimate was similar to that of 2004, but remained 45% above its long-term average. Total duck counts in southern Manitoba remained unchanged from the 2004 estimate and the long-term average

Several states and provinces conduct breeding waterfowl surveys in areas outside the geographic extent of the Waterfowl Breeding Population and Habitat Survey of the USFWS and CWS. In British Columbia, California, the northeastern U.S., Oregon, and Wisconsin, measures of precision for survey estimates are available. Total duck abundance

increased by 49% in California relative to 2004, and was similar to 2004 in British Columbia, Wisconsin, and the northeastern U.S. The total duck estimate was similar to the long-term average in California. In Wisconsin, total ducks were 73% above their long-term average. In British Columbia, California, and the northeastern U.S., total duck estimates were similar to their long-term averages. Of the states without measures of precision for total duck numbers, estimates of total ducks decreased in Nevada, Minnesota, Washington, Oregon, and Michigan, and increased in Nevada, relative to 2004.

Weather and habitat conditions during the summer months can influence waterfowl production. Good wetland conditions increase renesting effort and brood survival. In general, 2005 habitat conditions improved over most of the traditional survey area between May and July of 2005. Habitat in most of the prairies, especially southern Saskatchewan and eastern Montana improved between May and July because of abundant summer rain. Habitat conditions in the northern and eastern areas tend to be more stable because of the deeper, more permanent water bodies there. In general, the outlook for production was rated fair to good in the northern Prairie Provinces and good to excellent in the eastern survey area during 2005.

2006 Breeding Habitat Conditions, Populations, and Production

Overall Habitat and Population Status

Despite a very warm winter, breeding waterfowl habitat quality in the U.S. and Canada is slightly better this year than last year. Improvements in Canadian and U.S. prairie habitats were primarily due to average to above-average precipitation, warm spring temperatures, and carry-over effects from the good summer conditions of 2005. Improved habitat conditions were reflected in the higher number of ponds counted in Prairie Canada this year compared to last year. The 2006 estimate of ponds in Prairie Canada was 4.4 ± 0.2 million ponds, a 13% increase from last year's estimate of 3.9 ± 0.2 million ponds, and 32% above the 1955-2005 average (Table 1, Figure 1). The parkland and northern grassland regions of Manitoba and Saskatchewan received abundant rain in March and April, which created good to excellent habitat conditions. Higher water tables prevented farm activities in wetland basins and excellent residual nesting cover remained around many potholes. Many wetlands flooded beyond their normal basins and into surrounding uplands. Deeper water in permanent and semi-

Table 1. Estimated number (in thousands) of May ponds in portions of prairie and parkland Canada and the northcentral U.S.

Survey area	2006	2005	Change from 2005 %	Change from 2005 P	LTA [a]	Change from LTA %	Change from LTA P
Prairie Canada							
S. Alberta	996	750	+33	0.020	722	+38	<0.001
S. Saskatchewan	2,719	2,415	+13	0.250	1,963	+38	<0.001
S. Manitoba	735	755	-3	0.805	673	+9	0.351
Subtotal	4,450	3,921	+13	0.074	3,358	+32	<0.001
Northcentral U.S.							
Montana and Western Dakotas	615	663	-7	0.512	528	+16	0.064
Eastern Dakotas	1,030	798	+29	0.011	994	+4	0.625
Subtotal	1,644	1,461	+13	0.116	1,522	+8	0.159
Grand total	6,094	5,381	+13	0.025	4,830	+26	<0.001

[a]Long-term average. Prairie and parkland Canada, 1961-2005; northcentral U.S. and grand total, 1974-2005.

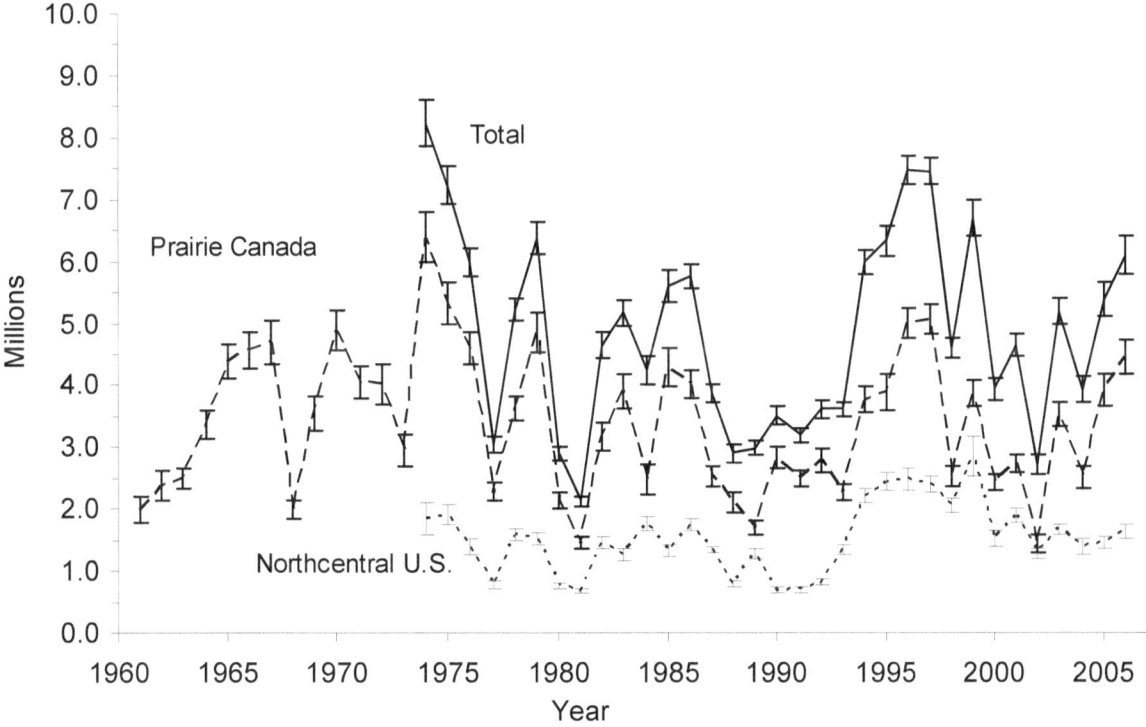

Figure 1. Number of ponds in May and 90% confidence intervals in prairie Canada and the northcentral U.S.

permanent wetlands, coupled with increased amounts of flooded emergent vegetation and woodland, likely benefited diving ducks and overwater- and cavity-nesting species. However, spring precipitation in the grasslands of southern Saskatchewan and extreme southwestern Manitoba was insufficient to fill seasonal and semi-permanent wetlands or create temporary wetlands for waterfowl, leaving these regions in fair or poor condition at the time of the survey. Above-average precipitation in the fall and spring in parts of southern Alberta improved conditions in this historically important pintail breeding region. This region has been dry since 1998, with the exception of 2003. However, central Alberta remained dry.

Habitat conditions on the U.S prairies were more variable than those on the Canadian prairies. The 2006 pond estimate for the north-central U.S. (1.6 ± 0.1 million) was similar to last year's estimate and the long-term average. The total pond estimate (Prairie Canada and U.S. combined) was 6.1 ± 0.2 million ponds. This was 13% greater than last year's estimate of 5.4 ± 0.2 million and 26% higher than the long-term average of 4.8 ± 0.1 million ponds. Habitat quality improved minimally in the easternmost regions of North and South Dakota relative to 2005. Small areas of the Eastern Dakotas were in good-to-excellent condition, helped by warm April temperatures and spring rains that advanced vegetation growth by about 2 weeks. However, most of the Drift Prairie, the Missouri Coteau, and the Coteau Slope remained in fair to poor condition due to lack of temporary and seasonal water and the deteriorated condition of semi-permanent basins. Permanent wetlands and dugouts were typically in various stages of recession. The Western Dakotas were generally in fair condition. Most wetland and upland habitats in Montana benefited modestly from average to above-average fall and winter precipitation and subsequent improvement in nesting habitat last year. Spring precipitation in Montana during March and April also helped mitigate several years of drought. Much of central Montana was in good condition due to ample late winter and early spring precipitation. Biologists there also noted improvements in upland vegetation over recent years. In the central region, most pond basins were full and stream systems were flowing. However, nesting habitat was generally fair to poor for most of the northern portion of Montana.

Habitat conditions in most northern regions of Canada were improved over last year due to an early ice break-up, warm spring temperatures, and good precipitation levels. In northern Saskatchewan, northern Manitoba, and western Ontario, winter snowfall was sufficient to recharge most beaver ponds and small lakes. Larger lakes and rivers tended to have higher water levels than in recent years. Conditions in the smaller wetlands were ideal. However, in northern Manitoba and northern Saskatchewan, some lakes associated with major rivers were flooded, with some flooded well into the surrounding upland vegetation. The potential for habitat loss due to flooding caused biologists to classify this region as good. In Alberta, water levels improved to the north, except for the Athabasca Delta, where wetlands, especially seasonal wetlands, generally had low water levels. Most of the Northwest Territories had good water levels. The exceptions were the southern portion, where heavy May rains flooded some nesting habitat, as well as a dry swath across the central part of the province. In contrast to most other northern areas and to the past few years, spring did not arrive early in Alaska this year. Overall, a normal spring phenology occurred throughout most of Alaska and the Yukon Territory, and ice persisted late in the following regions: the outer coast of the Yukon Delta, the northern Seward Peninsula, and on the Old Crow Flats. Some flooding occurred on a few major rivers. Overall, good waterfowl production was anticipated this year from the northwestern continental area, contingent on continued seasonal temperatures.

Spring-like conditions also arrived early in the East, with an early ice break-up and relatively mild temperatures. Biologists reported that habitat conditions were generally good across most of the survey area. Most regions had a warm, dry winter and a dry early spring. Extreme southern Ontario was relatively dry during the survey period and habitats were in fair to poor condition. However, precipitation after survey completion improved habitat conditions in this region. Abundant rain in May improved water levels in Maine, the Maritimes, southern Ontario, and Quebec, but caused some flooding in southern Ontario and Quebec and along the coast of Maine, New Brunswick, and Nova Scotia. In Quebec, a very early spring assured good habitat availability. Despite the early spring and the abundance of spring precipitation, a dry winter still left most of the marshes and rivers drier than in recent years. Many bogs were noticeably drier than recent years or dry entirely in a few cases. Winter precipitation increased to the west and north, which resulted in generally good water levels in central and northern Ontario. Conditions were good to excellent in central and northern Ontario due to the early spring phenology, generally good water levels, and warm spring temperatures.

In the traditional survey area, the total duck population estimate (excluding scoters, eiders, long-tailed ducks, mergansers, and wood ducks) was 36.2 ± 0.6 [SE] million birds. This was 14% greater than last year's estimate of 31.7 ± 0.6 million birds and 9% above the 1955-2005 long-term average (Table 2, Appendix G).

In the eastern Dakotas, total duck numbers were 12% higher than last year's estimate, and 23% above the long-term average. Counts in southern Alberta were 44% higher than last year's, and similar to their long-term average. The total-duck estimate increased 27% relative to last year in southern Saskatchewan and was 37% above the long-term average. The total duck count in southern Manitoba was similar to the 2005 estimate, but 16% above its long-term average. The total duck estimate in central and northern Alberta, northeastern British Columbia and the Northwest Territories was similar to that of 2005, and 28% below the long-term average (Table 2). The estimate in the northern Saskatchewan—northern Manitoba--western Ontario area was 16% below that of 2005, and 24% below the long-term average. Total ducks in the western Dakotas--Eastern Montana area were 48% above their 2005 estimate, and 18% above their long-term average. In the Alaska--Yukon Territory--Old Crow Flats region the total duck estimate was similar to that of 2005, but remained 34% above its long-term average.

Several states and provinces conduct breeding waterfowl surveys in areas outside the geographic extent of the Waterfowl Breeding Population and Habitat Survey of the USFWS and CWS. In British Columbia, California, the northeastern U.S., Oregon, and Wisconsin, measures of precision for survey estimates are available. Total duck estimates in California and the northeastern U.S. were similar to those of 2005 and to long-term averages. In Oregon, the total duck estimate was 17% higher than last year's, but 17% lower than the long-term average. In British Columbia, total duck numbers did not differ from their 2005 estimate, or their long-term average. In Wisconsin, the total duck estimate was 28% below last year's, but remained 22% above the long-term average. Of the states without measures of precision for total duck numbers, estimates of total ducks decreased in Minnesota and Michigan relative to 2005.

Trends and annual breeding population estimates for 10 principal duck species from the traditional survey area are provided in Figure 2, Tables 3-12, and Appendix F. Mallard abundance was 7.3 ± 0.2 million, which is similar to last year's estimate of 6.8 ± 0.3 million, and to the long-term average (Table 3). Mallard numbers were up 34% in southern Alberta relative to 2005, but remained 18% below the long-term average. In the Montana-Western Dakotas survey area, mallard counts were 76% higher than in 2005, and 36% higher than the long-tem mean. Mallard estimates were similar to 2005 estimates in the central and northern Alberta--northeastern British Columbia--Northwest Territories region, as well as the northern Saskatchewan--northern Manitoba--western Ontario survey area, but remained 49% and 43% below their long-term averages, respectively. Mallard numbers fell 27% since 2005, but remained 44% above their long-term average in the Alaska--Yukon Territory--Old Crow Flats region. In southern Manitoba and in the Eastern Dakotas, mallard counts were similar to last year's, but were 35% and 92% above their long-term averages, respectively. The mallard estimate was similar to last year's count, and 12% below the long-term average in southern Saskatchewan. In other areas where surveys are conducted and measures of precision for estimates are provided (the same states as for total ducks, as well as Michigan and Minnesota), mallard abundance remained unchanged from 2005, except for Minnesota (-33%) and Wisconsin (-31%). Mallard estimates were below the long-term average in Michigan (-50%), Oregon (-20%), and British Columbia (-26%), and similar to long-term averages in California, the northeastern U. S., and Wisconsin. Minnesota mallards were 28% below their long-term average, but a test statistic for this estimate was unavailable.

Blue-winged teal abundance was estimated at 5.9 ± 0.3 million birds, 28% higher than last year's estimate of 4.6 ± 0.2 million birds and 30% higher than the 1955-2005 average. Of the other duck species, gadwall (2.8 ± 0.2 million) were 30% higher than their 2005 estimate, and were 67% above their long-term average. American wigeon (2.2 ± 0.1 million) and scaup (3.2 ± 0.2 million) were similar to their 2005 estimates, but were 17% and 37% below their long-term averages, respectively. The green-winged teal (2.6 ± 0.2 million) estimate was 20% higher than last year's, and 39% higher than the long-term average. Northern pintails (3.4 ± 0.2 million) increased by 32% relative to last year, but remained 18% below their long-term average. The Northern shoveler (3.7 ± 0.2 million) estimate was similar to last year's, and 69% above the long-term average.

11

Table 2. Total duck[a] breeding population estimates (in thousands).

Region	2006	2005	Change from 2005		LTA[b]	Change from LTA	
			%	P		%	P
Traditional survey area							
Alaska - Yukon Territory - Old Crow Flats	4,755	5,114	-7	0.149	3,550	+34	<0.001
C. & N. Alberta - N.E. British Columbia - Northwest Territories	5,132	4,713	+9	0.222	7,153	-28	<0.001
N. Saskatchewan - N. Manitoba - W. Ontario	2,711	3,223	-16	0.047	3,557	-24	<0.001
S. Alberta	4,581	3,178	+44	<0.001	4,283	+7	0.121
S. Saskatchewan	10,096	7,967	+27	<0.001	7,348	+37	<0.001
S. Manitoba	1,796	1,627	+10	0.137	1,544	+16	0.003
Montana and Western Dakotas	1,910	1,290	+48	<0.001	1,613	+18	0.001
Eastern Dakotas	5,181	4,623	+12	0.073	4,201	+23	<0.001
Total	36,160	31,735	+14	<0.001	33,251	+9	<0.001
Other regions							
British Columbia[c]	8	6	+40	0.252	6	+22	0.385
California	649	615	+6	0.719	599	-8	0.507
Northeastern U.S.[d]	1,392	1,416	-2	0.865	1,429	-3	0.719
Oregon	263	225	+17	0.061	295	-11	0.016
Wisconsin	523	724	-28	0.022	429	+22	0.072

[a] Excludes eider, long-tailed duck, wood duck, scoter, and merganser in traditional survey area; excludes eider, long-tailed duck, wood duck, redhead, canvasback and ruddy duck in eastern survey area; species composition for other regions varies.
[b] Long-term average. Traditional survey area 1955-2005; years for other regions vary (see Appendix E).
[c] Index to waterfowl use in prime waterfowl producing regions of the province.
[d] Includes all or portions of CT, DE, MD, MA, NH, NJ, NY, PA, RI, VT, and VA.

Table 3. Mallard breeding population estimates (in thousands).

Region	2006	2005	Change from 2005 %	Change from 2005 P	LTA[b]	Change from LTA %	Change from LTA P
Traditional survey area							
Alaska - Yukon Territory - Old Crow Flats	516	703	-27	0.009	357	+44	0.001
C. & N. Alberta - N.E. British Columbia - Northwest Territories	558	533	+5	0.818	1,086	-49	<0.001
N. Saskatchewan - N. Manitoba - W. Ontario	656	937	-30	0.116	1,159	-43	<0.001
S. Alberta	901	671	+34	0.006	1,099	-18	<0.001
S. Saskatchewan	1,832	1,729	+6	0.530	2,072	-12	0.021
S. Manitoba	511	455	+12	0.351	378	+35	0.004
Montana and Western Dakotas	679	387	+76	<0.001	499	+36	0.002
Eastern Dakotas	1,624	1,340	+21	0.140	846	+92	<0.001
Total	7,277	6,755	+8	0.147	7,496	-3	0.338
Eastern survey area	371	402	-7	b	364	+1	b
Other regions							
British Columbia[c]	<1	<1	-6	0.688	<1	-26	<0.001
California	399	318	+26	0.270	372	-7	0.667
Michigan	208	230	-10	0.630	414	-50	<0.001
Minnesota	161	239	-33	0.038	223	-28	e
Northeastern U.S.[d]	725	754	-4	0.693	800	-9	0.136
Oregon	88	83	+6	0.598	110	-20	0.003
Wisconsin	219	317	-31	0.064	179	+22	0.193

[a] Long-term average. Traditional survey area 1955-2005; eastern survey area 1990-2005; years for other regions vary (see Appendix E).
[b] P-values not appropriate because these data were analyzed with Bayesian methods.
[c] Index to waterfowl use in prime waterfowl producing regions of the province.
[d] Includes all or portions of CT, DE, MD, MA, NH, NJ, NY, PA, RI, VT, and VA.
[e] Value for test statistic was not available.

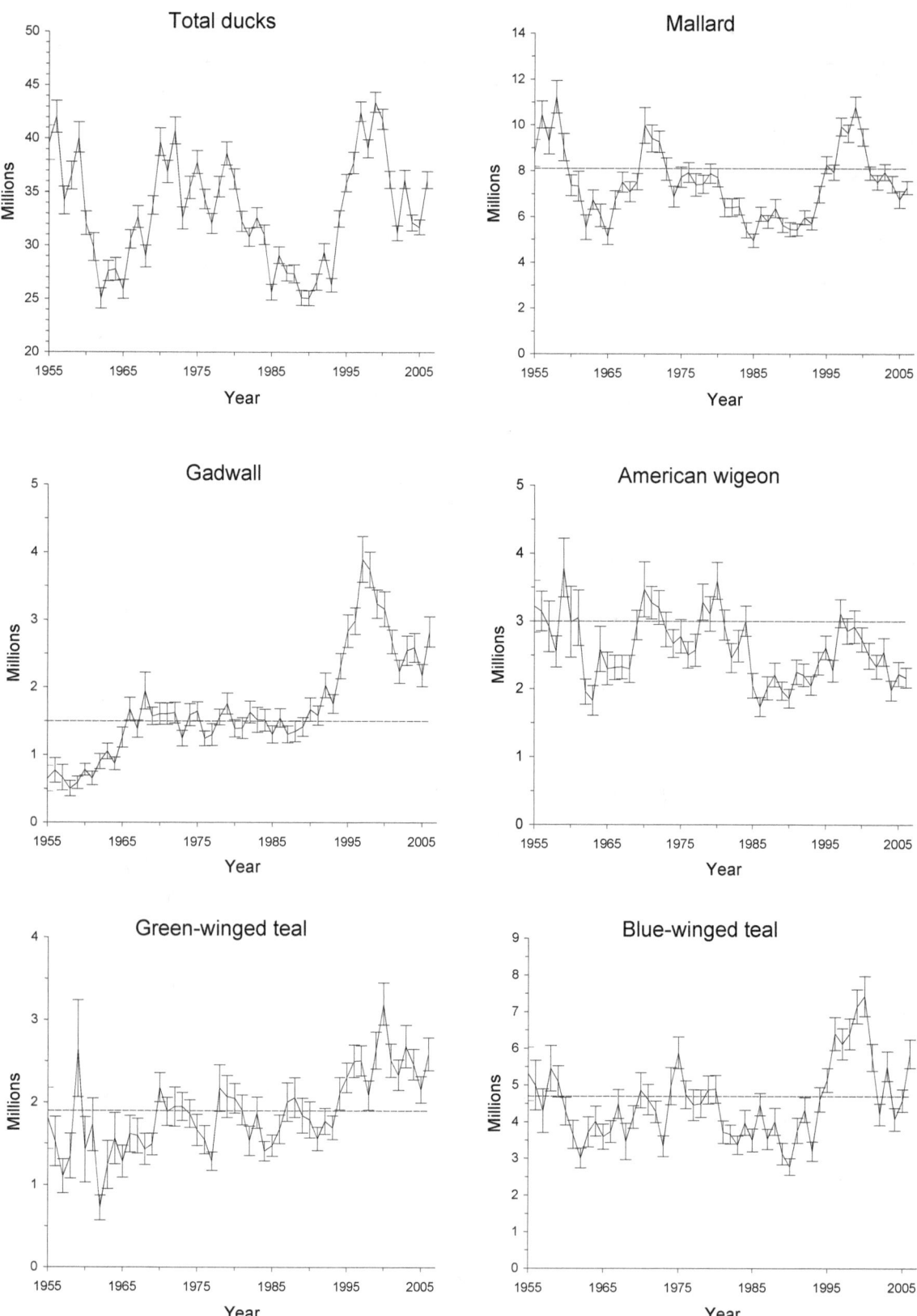

Figure 2. Breeding population estimates, 90% confidence intervals, and North American Waterfowl Management Plan population goal (dashed line) for selected species in the traditional survey area (strata 1-18, 20-50, 75-77).

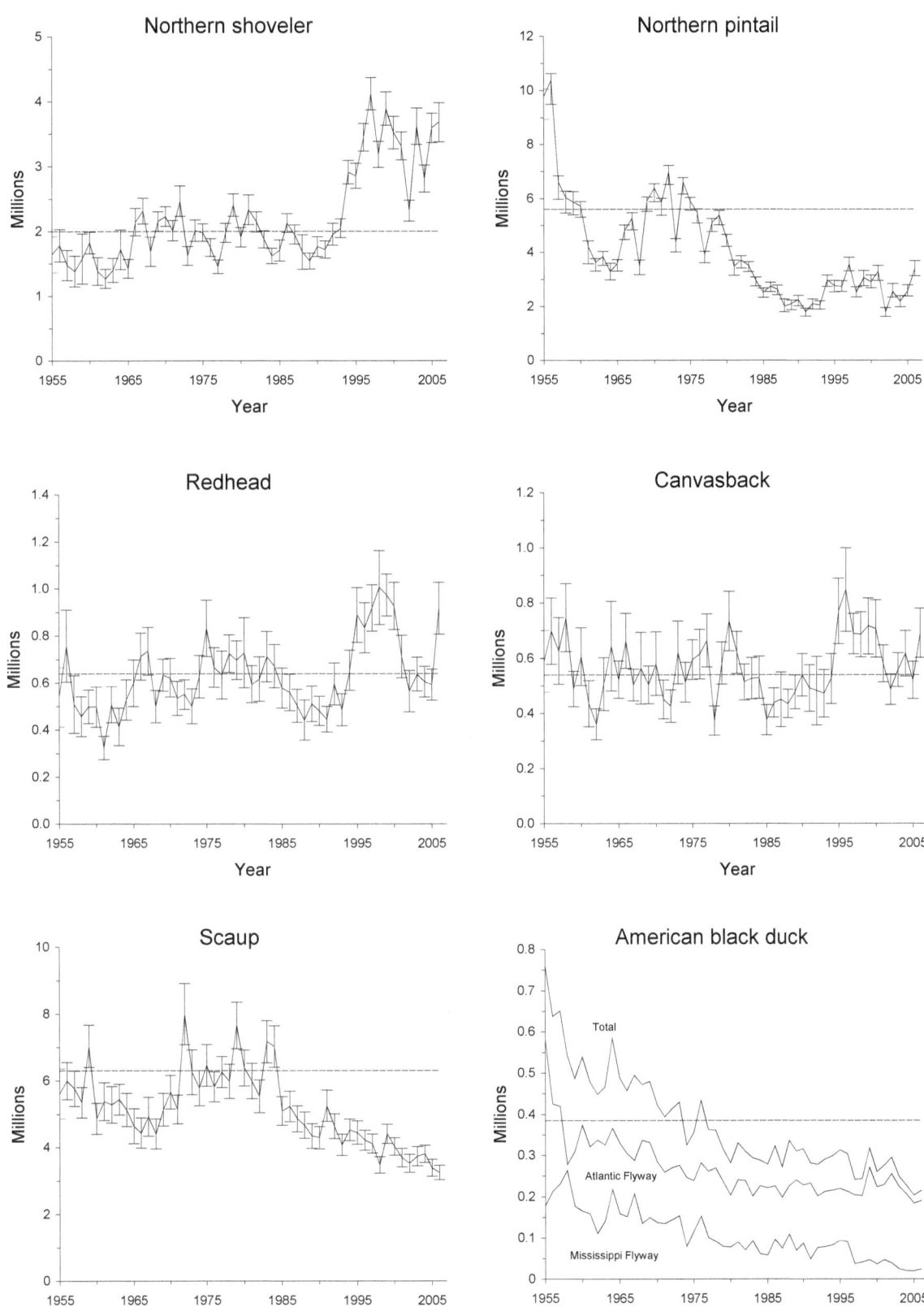

Figure 2 (continued).

Redhead (0.9 ± 0.1 million), and canvasback (0.7 ± 0.1 million) estimates were 55% and 33% above their 2005 estimates and 47% and 23% above long-term averages, respectively.

Populations of the 10 most abundant species in the eastern survey area were all similar to their 1990-2005 estimates (Table 13, Figures 3 and 4, Appendix H). American wigeon and buffleheads were 51% and 58% below their 2005 estimates, respectively. Estimates of all other species in the survey area were similar to last year's estimates.

The longest time-series of data available to assess the status of the American black duck (*Anas rubripes*) is provided by the midwinter surveys conducted in January in states of the Atlantic and Mississippi Flyways. The trend in the winter index for the total population is depicted in Figure 2. Measures of precision are not available for the midwinter surveys. Midwinter counts of American black ducks (214,800) in both flyways combined) increased 5% relative to 2005 counts (203,900), but remained 18% lower than the 10-year mean (261,700). In the Atlantic Flyway, the midwinter index of 190,700 increased 4% from 184,100 in 2005, and was 14% below the most recent 10-year mean (221,500). In the Mississippi Flyway, the American black duck mid-winter index increased 22% from 19,900 in 2005 to 24,200, which is 40% below the 10-year mean (40,300). A shorter time series for assessing change in American black duck population status is provided by the breeding waterfowl surveys conducted by the USFWS and CWS in the eastern survey area. In the eastern survey area, the 2005 estimate for breeding American black ducks (490,000) was similar to the 2005 estimate (472,000) and to the 1990-2005 average (458,000).

Trends in wood duck populations are monitored by the North American Breeding Bird Survey (BBS), a series of roadside routes surveyed during May and June each year. Wood ducks are encountered with low frequency along BBS routes, limiting the amount and quality of available information for analysis (Sauer and Droege 1990). However, the BBS provides the only long-term indices of this species' regional populations. Trend analysis suggests that wood duck numbers have increased 3.7% per year over the entire survey period (1966-2005) and 2.0% over the past 20 years (1986-2005), in the Atlantic and Mississippi Flyways combined. Specifically, for the Atlantic Flyway, the BBS indicated a 4.6% annual increase in wood ducks over the entire 40 years of the survey (1966-2005), and a 2.6% annual increase over the past 20 years (1986-2005). In the Mississippi Flyway, the 40-year BBS trend indicated a 3.1% annual increase, and although the slope of the 20-year trend is positive, it is not statistically significant. Analysis of wood duck BBS data over the past 10-year period (1996-2005) yielded no significant short-term trend for the Atlantic or Mississippi Flyways, or the two flyways combined (J. Sauer, U. S. Geological Survey/Biological Resources Division, unpublished data).

Weather and habitat conditions during the summer months can influence waterfowl production. Good wetland conditions increase renesting effort and brood survival. In general, 2006 July habitat conditions over most of the traditional survey area were similar to those observed in May. While no formal July surveys were flown this year, experienced crew leaders in Montana and the western Dakotas, the eastern Dakotas, southern Alberta, and southern Saskatchewan returned to their May survey areas in early July to qualitatively assess habitat changes between May and July. Biologists from other survey areas communicated with local biologists to get their impressions of 2006 waterfowl production and monitored weather conditions. Habitat over most of the prairies remained stable between May and July because of adequate summer rain. The exception was the eastern Dakotas survey area, where wetland conditions deteriorated. Habitat conditions in the northern and eastern areas tend to be more stable because of the deeper, more permanent water bodies there. In general, the outlook for production was rated fair to good in the northern Prairie Provinces and good to excellent in the eastern survey area.

Regional Habitat and Population Status

A description of habitat conditions, populations, and production for each for the major breeding areas follows. More detailed reports of specific regions are available in *Waterfowl Population Surveys* reports, located on the Division of Migratory Bird Management's home page. Some of the habitat information that follows was taken from those reports (http://www.fws.gov/migratorybirds/reports/reports.html).

Southern Alberta: The outlook for this crew area (strata 26-29, 75-76) was much improved over recent years. Precipitation during June was generally much above normal in the southern plains of Alberta and in the northwest corner of the province, and below to much below normal in north-central Alberta. Precipitation elsewhere was generally below normal to normal.

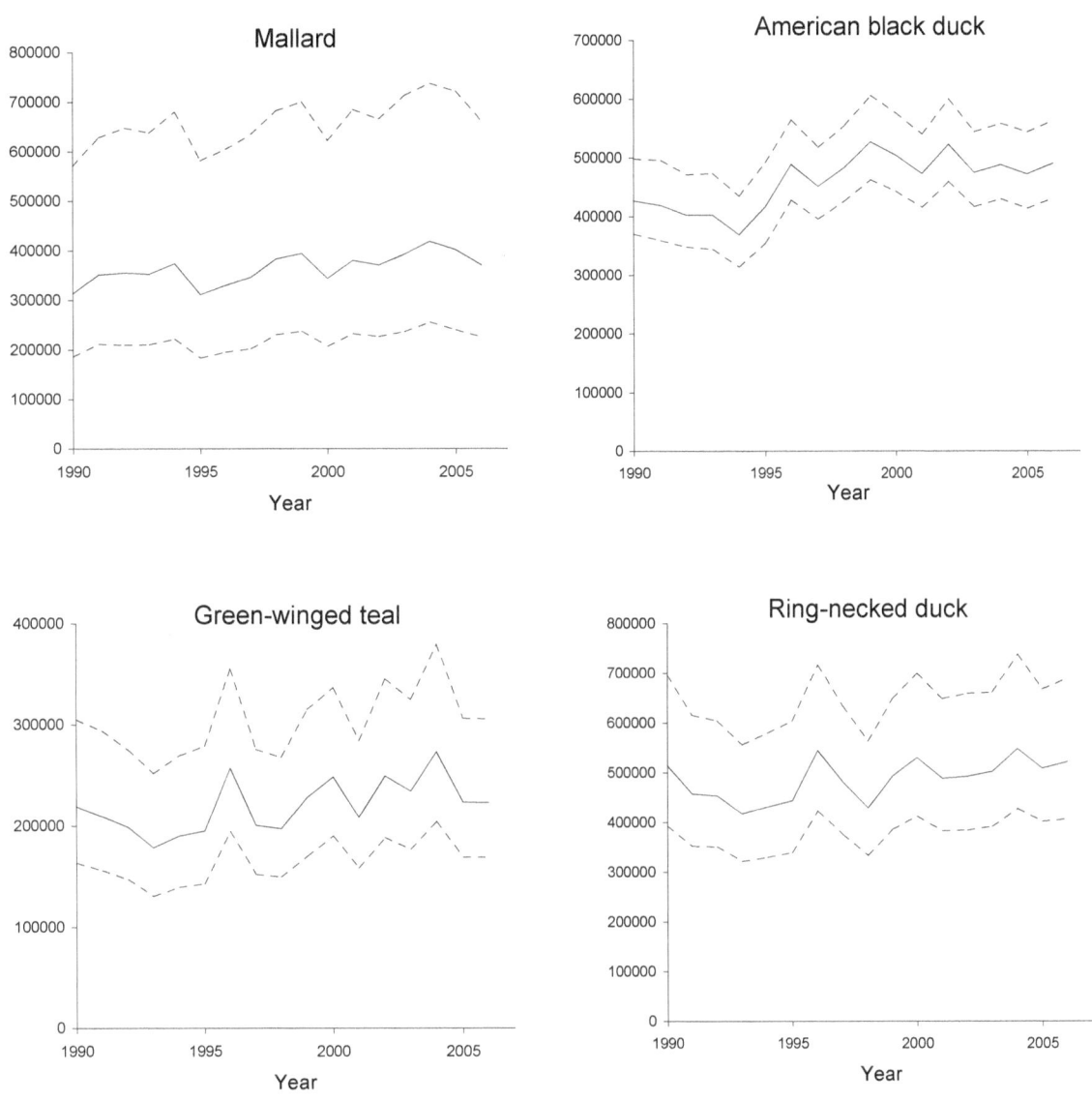

Figure 3. Breeding population estimates (from Bayesian hierarchical models) and 95% credibility intervals for selected species in the eastern survey area (strata 51, 52, 63, 64, 66-68, 70-72).

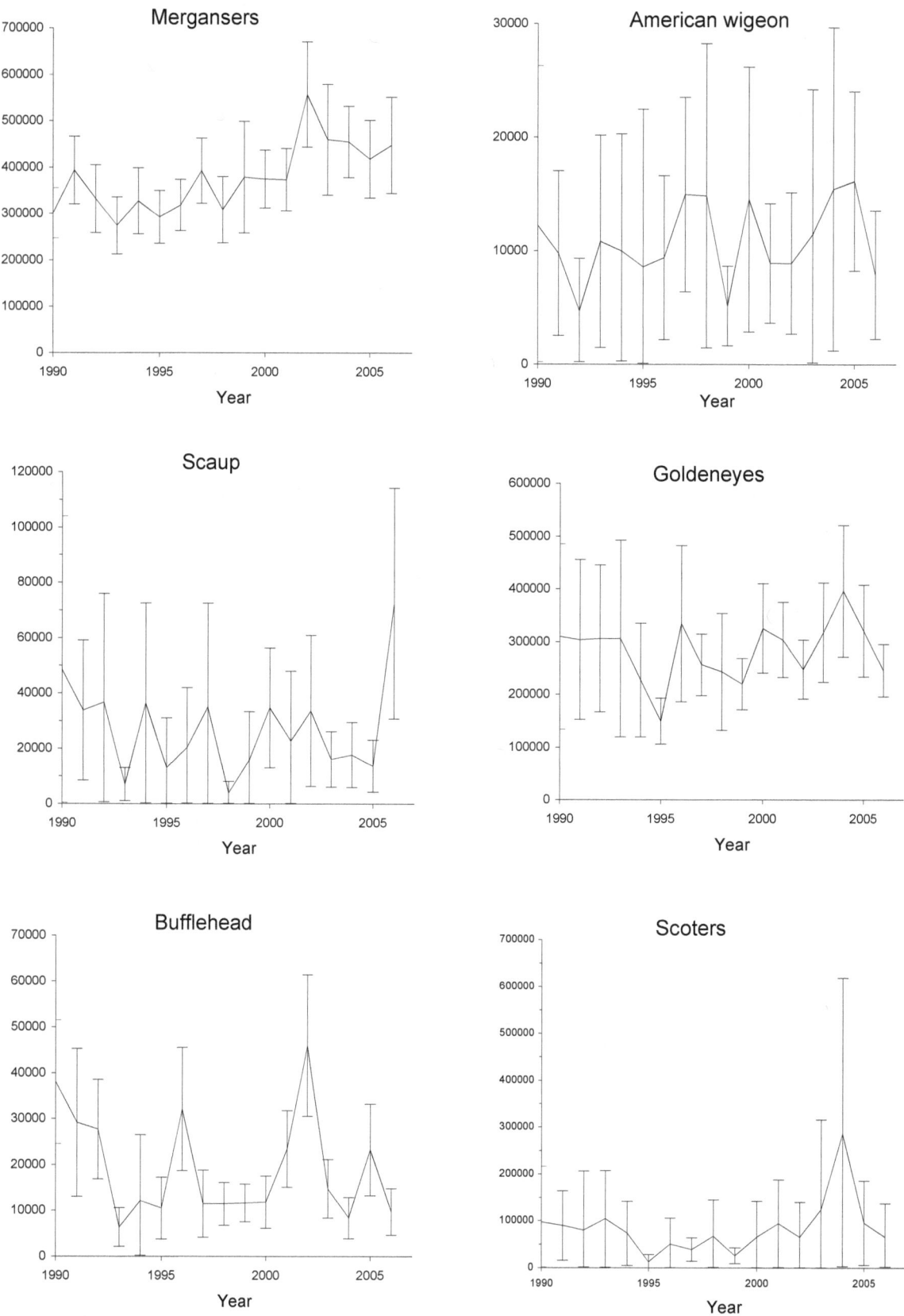

Figure 4. Breeding population estimates (harmonic means) and 95% confidence intervals for selected species in the eastern survey area (strata 51, 52, 63, 64, 66-68, 70-72).

Table 4. Gadwall breeding population estimates (in thousands) for regions in the traditional survey area.

Region	2006	2005	Change from 2005		LTA	Change from LTA	
			%	P		%	P
Alaska-Yukon Territory – Old Crow Flats	2	3	-29	0.739	2	0	0.998
C. & N. Alberta – N.E. British Columbia - Northwest Territories	135	77	+75	0.102	47	+187	0.006
N. Saskatchewan- N. Manitoba - W. Ontario	16	19	-14	0.747	27	-41	0.042
S. Alberta	455	338	+35	0.152	309	+47	0.010
S. Saskatchewan	1,202	723	+66	0.006	556	+116	<0.001
S. Manitoba	125	120	+4	0.820	67	+88	<0.001
Montana and Western Dakotas	216	187	+16	0.474	194	+11	0.476
Eastern Dakotas	673	712	-6	0.642	491	+37	<0.001
Total	2,825	2,179	+30	0.003	1,692	+67	<0.001

Table 5. American wigeon breeding population estimates (in thousands) for regions in the traditional survey area.

Region	2006	2005	Change from 2005		LTA	Change from LTA	
			%	P		%	P
Alaska-Yukon Territory – Old Crow Flats	822	873	-6	0.552	511	+61	<0.001
C. & N. Alberta – N.E. British Columbia - Northwest Territories	570	583	-2	0.921	912	-38	<0.001
N. Saskatchewan- N. Manitoba - W. Ontario	105	174	-40	0.080	253	-58	<0.001
S. Alberta	189	125	+50	0.025	296	-36	<0.001
S. Saskatchewan	282	294	-4	0.845	425	-34	<0.001
S. Manitoba	16	34	-53	0.086	62	-74	<0.001
Montana and Western Dakotas	120	67	+79	0.008	109	+10	0.531
Eastern Dakotas	67	73	-8	0.767	48	+39	0.140
Total	2,171	2,225	-2	0.766	2,617	-17	<0.001

Table 6. Green-winged teal breeding population estimates (in thousands) for regions in the traditional survey area.

Region	2006	2005	Change from 2005		LTA	Change from LTA	
			%	P		%	P
Alaska-Yukon Territory – Old Crow Flats	780	713	+9	0.471	358	+118	<0.001
C. & N. Alberta – N.E. British Columbia - Northwest Territories	751	437	+72	0.018	752	0	0.990
N. Saskatchewan- N. Manitoba - W. Ontario	303	310	-2	0.896	197	+54	0.001
S. Alberta	178	159	+12	0.720	194	-8	0.709
S. Saskatchewan	401	359	+12	0.632	230	+75	0.007
S. Manitoba	65	55	+19	0.448	52	+27	0.215
Montana and Western Dakotas	34	83	-59	0.005	40	-15	0.364
Eastern Dakotas	75	42	+81	0.164	45	+67	0.164
Total	2,587	2,157	+20	0.031	1,867	+39	<0.001

Table 7. Blue-winged teal breeding population estimates (in thousands) for regions in the traditional survey area.

Region	2006	2005	Change from 2005		LTA	Change from LTA	
			%	P		%	P
Alaska-Yukon Territory – Old Crow Flats	0	3	-100	0.339	1	-100	<0.001
C. & N. Alberta – N.E. British Columbia - Northwest Territories	316	247	+28	0.456	270	+17	0.515
N. Saskatchewan- N. Manitoba - W. Ontario	82	139	-41	0.237	265	-69	<0.001
S. Alberta	864	649	+33	0.126	609	+42	0.015
S. Saskatchewan	2,228	1,597	+40	0.019	1,218	+83	<0.001
S. Manitoba	426	339	+26	0.117	382	+11	0.329
Montana and Western Dakotas	346	286	+21	0.240	263	+32	0.047
Eastern Dakotas	1,598	1,325	+21	0.171	1,492	+7	0.418
Total	5,860	4,586	+28	0.001	4,501	+30	<0.001

Table 8. Northern shoveler breeding population estimates (in thousands) for regions in the traditional survey area.

| Region | 2006 | 2005 | Change from 2005 | | LTA | Change from LTA | |
			%	P		%	P
Alaska-Yukon Territory – Old Crow Flats	409	666	-39	0.003	267	+53	0.002
C. & N. Alberta – N.E. British Columbia - Northwest Territories	193	213	-10	0.690	213	-10	0.498
N. Saskatchewan- N. Manitoba - W. Ontario	12	29	-59	0.016	43	-72	<0.001
S. Alberta	701	548	+28	0.190	360	+95	<0.001
S. Saskatchewan	1,612	1,314	+23	0.210	648	+149	<0.001
S. Manitoba	178	211	-16	0.430	107	+66	<0.001
Montana and Western Dakotas	163	148	+10	0.612	149	+9	0.514
Eastern Dakotas	414	464	-11	0.477	389	+6	0.594
Total	3,680	3,591	+2	0.765	2,177	+69	<0.001

Table 9. Northern pintail breeding population estimates (in thousands) for regions in the traditional survey area.

| Region | 2006 | 2005 | Change from 2005 | | LTA | Change from LTA | |
			%	P		%	P
Alaska-Yukon Territory – Old Crow Flats	1,041	905	+15	0.310	913	+14	0.174
C. & N. Alberta – N.E. British Columbia - Northwest Territories	126	108	+16	0.662	378	-67	<0.001
N. Saskatchewan- N. Manitoba - W. Ontario	6	8	-31	0.470	41	-86	<0.001
S. Alberta	611	282	+116	<0.001	721	-15	0.107
S. Saskatchewan	1,024	858	+19	0.343	1,218	-16	0.203
S. Manitoba	57	68	-16	0.480	112	-49	<0.001
Montana and Western Dakotas	264	75	+252	<0.001	269	-2	0.907
Eastern Dakotas	257	256	+1	0.968	459	-44	<0.001
Total	3,386	2,561	+32	0.001	4,111	-18	<0.001

Table 10. Redhead breeding population estimates (in thousands) for regions in the traditional survey area.

| Region | 2006 | 2005 | Change from 2005 | | LTA | Change from LTA | |
			%	P		%	P
Alaska-Yukon Territory – Old Crow Flats	10	<1	+4000	0.106	1	+622	0.154
C. & N. Alberta – N.E. British Columbia - Northwest Territories	59	49	+19	0.679	38	+54	0.143
N. Saskatchewan- N. Manitoba - W. Ontario	5	13	-61	0.050	28	-82	<0.001
S. Alberta	154	91	+69	0.074	116	+33	0.214
S. Saskatchewan	435	226	+93	0.007	190	+129	0.001
S. Manitoba	102	98	+4	0.903	72	+42	0.127
Montana and Western Dakotas	12	3	+315	0.054	9	+25	0.573
Eastern Dakotas	139	112	+25	0.389	169	-17	0.284
Total	916	592	+55	0.001	624	+47	0.001

Table 11. Canvasback breeding population estimates (in thousands) for regions in the traditional survey area.

| Region | 2006 | 2005 | Change from 2005 | | LTA | Change from LTA | |
			%	P		%	P
Alaska-Yukon Territory – Old Crow Flats	73	95	-23	0.542	91	-20	0.475
C. & N. Alberta – N.E. British Columbia - Northwest Territories	109	98	+12	0.771	73	+50	0.177
N. Saskatchewan- N. Manitoba - W. Ontario	13	39	-67	0.068	55	-77	<0.001
S. Alberta	76	43	+79	0.105	64	+20	0.440
S. Saskatchewan	287	162	+76	0.026	182	+57	0.037
S. Manitoba	87	48	+84	0.166	56	+56	0.221
Montana and Western Dakotas	12	5	+157	0.121	8	+58	0.321
Eastern Dakotas	33	31	+5	0.875	33	0	1.000
Total	691	521	+33	0.051	562	+23	0.067

Table 12. Scaup (greater and lesser scaup combined) breeding population estimates (in thousands) for regions in the traditional survey area.

Region	2006	2005	Change from 2005		LTA	Change from LTA	
			%	P		%	P
Alaska-Yukon Territory – Old Crow Flats	884	961	-8	0.500	915	-3	0.680
C. & N. Alberta – N.E. British Columbia - Northwest Territories	1,169	1,361	-14	0.316	2,627	-55	<0.001
N. Saskatchewan- N. Manitoba - W. Ontario	335	349	-4	0.816	587	-43	<0.001
S. Alberta	214	127	+69	0.071	353	-39	0.001
S. Saskatchewan	391	381	+3	0.918	416	-6	0.714
S. Manitoba	97	60	+61	0.146	135	-28	0.103
Montana and Western Dakotas	19	16	+14	0.723	53	-65	<0.001
Eastern Dakotas	138	132	+5	0.854	97	+42	0.097
Total	3,247	3,387	-4	0.586	5,184	-37	<0.001

Table 13. Duck breeding population estimates [a] (in thousands) for the 10 most abundant species in the eastern survey area.

Species	2006	2005	% Change from 2005	Average [b]	% Change from average
Mergansers (common, red-breasted, and hooded)	448	418	+7	373	+20
Mallard	371	402	-7	364	+1
American black duck	490	472	+4	458	+7
American wigeon	8	16	-51[c]	11	-28
Green-winged teal	223	223	<1%	219	+2
Scaup (greater and lesser)	72	14	+428	24	+198
Ring-necked duck	522	509	+2	484	+7
Goldeneyes (common and Barrow's)	246	320	-23	285	-14
Bufflehead	10	23	-58[c]	20	-51
Scoters (black and surf)	65	96	-32	86	-24

[a] Estimates for mallards, American black ducks, green-winged teal, and ring-necked duck from Bayesian hierarchical analysis using FWS and CWS data from strata 51, 52, 63, 64, 66-68, 70-72. All others were computed as harmonic means of FWS and CWS estimates for strata 51, 52, 63, 64, 66-68, 70-72.

[b] Average for 1990-2005.

[c] Significance (P<0.05) determined by non-overlap of Bayesian credibility intervals or confidence intervals.

Overall, May ponds were up 33% relative to 2005, and 38% above their long-term average. In response, total duck (+44%) and Northern pintail (+116%) numbers were considerably higher than in 2005, and were similar to their long-term averages. Mallard (+34%), American wigeon (+50%), and scaup (+69%) estimates were much higher than those of 2005, but these species remained 18%, 36%, and 39% below their long-term averages, respectively. Northern shoveler, gadwall, and blue-winged teal estimates were all similar to 2005 estimates, but these species were 95%, 47%, and 42% above their long-term averages for the survey area, respectively. The redhead estimate was 69% higher than last year's, but similar to its long-term average. Green-winged teal and canvasback estimates were similar to their 2005 counts and long-term averages.

Precipitation during May and June was below normal to normal, except in most southern plains areas and some areas of northwest Alberta where it has been above to much above normal. Habitat conditions in July remained similar to conditions in May. Precipitation in June kept pond levels high, which predicted good brood production. Some areas in eastern stratum 26 actually improved from May to July.

Southern Saskatchewan: During the 2006 survey, Southern Saskatchewan generally had poor to fair waterfowl habitat in the southern grasslands and good to excellent waterfowl habitat in the northern grasslands and Parkland region. Spring runoff was below average in the southwest, southeast, and northwest and above average in the northeast and central regions of the grainbelt. Flooding of fields, roads, and houses occurred in May and early June in this region.

The grasslands strata of 32 and 33 received below average to average winter precipitation, except in the Cypress Hills, where precipitation was above average (Agriculture and Agri-food Canada 2006). Spring precipitation increased across the southern grasslands, but not to the extent necessary to fill seasonal and semi-permanent wetlands or create ephemeral or temporary wetlands for waterfowl. Upland habitat conditions throughout the southern grasslands appeared to be in fair to good condition for nesting ducks.

The Parklands (stratum 30-31) received average to above average precipitation during the winter and spring and both upland nesting cover and wetlands were in good to excellent condition

(Agriculture and Agri-food Canada 2006). Many wetlands flooded beyond their normal basins and into the surrounding uplands. There was also an increase in flooded emergent vegetation and woodland, which likely benefited overwater and cavity nesting species.

The May pond estimate was similar to last year's, and was 38% above the long-term average. Total ducks were 27% above the 2005 estimate, and 37% higher than their long-term average. Mallard and American wigeon estimates were similar to those of 2005, but were 12% and 34% below their long-term averages, respectively. Northern shoveler numbers were also similar to last year's, but were 149% above the long-term average. Gadwall (+66%, +116% LTA), blue-winged teal (+40%, +83% LTA), redhead (+93%, +129% LTA), and canvasback (+76%, +57% LTA) estimates were all well above those of 2005, and their long-term averages. Northern pintail and scaup estimates were similar to last year's, and to their long-term averages.

In a typical year in southern Saskatchewan, 40-60% of the wetlands present in May dry up by July. However, this July, wetland abundance was similar to that seen in May, which was expected to provide abundant habitat and cover for waterfowl broods. Habitat conditions in the grasslands strata (32 and 33) changed little from May. The western and southern portions of the grasslands remained dry, and potential for waterfowl production and recruitment was still rated poor to fair. Good nesting and wetland habitat existed across the central parts of the grasslands, including the Missouri Coteau. Sheetwater was still present across the northern and northwestern grasslands and most wetlands had flooded emergent vegetation. The northern grasslands continued to have excellent upland and wetland habitat conditions for waterfowl nesting and brood rearing. Likewise, the northwest Parklands (stratum 30) changed little since May. Good to excellent waterfowl production and recruitment was expected from this stratum. Conditions in the northeast Parklands (stratum 31) also remained unchanged, with very good upland habitat for waterfowl nesting. The western two-thirds of the stratum had excellent wetland habitat for brood rearing. However, the eastern third of the stratum was drier and wetland conditions were only fair to good. Southeastern Saskatchewan, although drier (poor to fair) south in Stratum 35, was wetter (good to excellent) to the north in Stratum 34. Overall, the survey area was rated good-excellent for re-nesting potential and duckling production.

Southern Manitoba: After one of the warmest winters on record, southern Manitoba (strata 24, 36-40) received substantial amounts of precipitation during March and April. Runoff was substantial and thousands of acres of cropland were flooded in the Red and Assiniboine River Valleys of the central and eastern portions of the area. Strata 38, 39, and 40 of the southwestern portions of Manitoba saw substantially improved nesting cover and similar wetland numbers relative to the good wetland conditions of 2005. Higher water tables prevented farm activities in wetland basins, so excellent residual nesting cover remained around potholes. Excellent conditions prevailed where these wetlands were associated with natural grasslands. By contrast, the far southwestern corner of Manitoba had much less precipitation compared to areas just to the northeast. Winter snow and spring rains were virtually nonexistent and pothole numbers appeared lower than in 2005. Dry conditions have prevailed there for the last 2-3 years, which rendered habitat poor for nesting waterfowl. In the west-central portion of the Province (Strata 25, 36 and 37) conditions were notably drier, but still appeared better than in the previous 3–4 years. Strata 36 and 37 received substantially less rainfall and are drier than areas further south, but nesting cover still was better than average. The Saskatchewan River area (Stratum 25) had higher than average water levels which likely favored diving ducks over dabbling ducks. Biologists observed more divers but fewer dabblers than usual in the area, as the high water produced good nesting habitat for overwater-nesting diving ducks, but probably prevented high densities of dabblers from successfully breeding.

The May pond count was similar to the 2005 estimate and to the long-term average. Green-winged teal, blue-winged teal, redheads, canvasbacks, and lesser scaup were similar to their 2005 estimates and long-term averages. Total ducks, mallards, and Northern shovelers were similar to their 2005 estimates, but 16%, 35%, and 66% above their long-term averages, respectively. Northern pintail estimates were similar to those of 2005, but remained 49% below the long-term average. The gadwall estimate was unchanged relative to last year, and was 88% above the long-term average. The American wigeon estimate was 53% lower than last year's, and remained 74% below the long-term average for the survey area.

Good May habitat conditions persisted into July due to average precipitation that helped wetlands retain their value for waterfowl. In southeastern Manitoba (Stratum 38) sporadic rain during June kept up with evaporation loss. Although these wetlands are not exceptional habitat relative to the rest of the survey area, (even when wet), they remained in fair to good condition as of July. In southwestern (Stratum 39) and the central (Stratum 40) Manitoba brood habitat was good to excellent, as many wetlands persisted due to their excellent condition during May. The north central areas (Stratum 36 and 37) were only in fair condition for duckling production. Residual vegetation from 2005 appeared to pay off in good nest success, and survival of dabbler ducklings should be good, due to the availability of good brood rearing habitat. For the second year in a row, permanent wetlands in Stratum 39 and 40 had good water depths and excellent emergent vegetation, which likely benefited diving duck production. Overall, good duck brood production was predicted in southern Manitoba.

Montana and Western Dakotas: Eastern Montana north of the Missouri River (Stratum 41) experienced a relatively mild winter with above-normal summer and fall precipitation. In addition to rain and snow in March and April, this further mitigated the effects of several years of drought. However, even in wet years, the path and speed of spring storm tracks typically produces a complex mosaic of variable habitat quality in the Eastern Montana-Western Dakotas survey area. In contrast to the past several years, in northeast Montana near Plentywood wetland conditions were poor and spring vegetation growth was sparse. A large central portion of stratum 41 bounded by Lewistown, Malta, and the North Dakota border had above-average habitat conditions, though in the far northwest portion of the stratum, conditions were fair to poor. In eastern Montana south of the Missouri River (Stratum 42), conditions were average throughout most of the region, with above average conditions in the southeast. In particular, the area between Lewistown and Glendive had good habitat, as did the region east from Billings to the Dakota border, which is usually dry. In the western Dakotas (strata 43 and 44) conditions were average to below average.

Overall in Montana and the Western Dakotas, May pond counts were similar to the 2005 estimate, and 16% higher than the long-term average. Total ducks were 48% higher than their 2005 estimate, and 18% above their long-term average. Mallard numbers were also up, 76% higher than last year's estimate, and 36% above the long-term average. American wigeon (+79%)

Northern pintails (+252%), and redheads (+315%) were well above their 2005 estimates, but similar to their long-term averages for the survey area. Green-winged teal numbers were 59% lower than last year's estimate, but similar to their long-term average. The blue-winged teal estimate was similar to last year's, and remained 32% above the long-term average. The scaup estimate was similar to last year's, and remained 65% below the long term average. Gadwall, Northern shoveler, and canvasback estimates were similar to those of 2005, and to long-term averages.

In July, Eastern Montana and the western Dakotas generally continued to reflect improved waterfowl habitat quality relative to the previous several years. Brood numbers reflected a generally successful nesting season in most areas and for the most part, class II broods were observed. Some class I broods were also observed, which suggested that late nesting and renesting had also occurred. Conditions in the northern portion of eastern Montana (Stratum 41) were generally similar to those recorded in May. The region east of Cut Bank, west of Havre and north of Great Falls remained poor with many dry basins and dry or fragmented stream channels. Stratum 42 habitat quality was quite variable. The southeastern region near Broadus and west to Billings continued to have surprisingly favorable water and brood habitat conditions, while the central portion of the stratum was drier than in May. Stratum 43 (western North Dakota) conditions were largely unchanged since May, with only fair habitat observed from the Montana/North Dakota border to within 30 miles of the Missouri River. In western South Dakota (Stratum 44), the general trend in July was a gradation of production habitat from fair in the west to poor in the east.

Eastern Dakotas: Last winter was generally mild, with less than average precipitation in eastern North and South Dakota (Strata 45-49). The wettest areas spanned the northern tier of counties in ND from the Turtle Mountains east to the Minnesota border, as well as a swath south through statum 47 to the southeastern corner of South Dakota. Conditions were especially favorable in the northeastern corner of South Dakota, which received good winter precipitation and was the only portion of the crew area rated excellent. However, much of the drift prairie in South Dakota and the Coteau Slope in North Dakota remained poor. Overall, wetland conditions were improved compared to last year's

dry conditions. Although duck numbers in the crew area were good, and vegetation development was 2-3 weeks earlier than normal, in the aggregate, the habitat in this crew area was fair as of May 2006.

May ponds were 29% higher than the 2005 estimate, and similar to the long-term average. The total duck estimate was 12% higher than the 2005 count and 23% above the long-term average. 2006 estimates for all of the major duck species in this crew area were similar to last year's estimates. Mallard numbers were 92% above their long-term average. Gadwall (+37%) and scaup (+42%) remained above their long-term averages for the area. Pintail numbers were 44% below their long-term average. American wigeon, green-winged teal, blue-winged teal, Northern shoveler, redhead, and canvasback estimates were all similar to their long-term averages.

Wetland conditions in the survey area deteriorated between May and July of 2006. During June and the first half of July, temperatures were average to above average in the eastern Dakotas. There was little precipitation, which added further to the deterioration of habitat conditions observed in May. During July reconnaissance flights, over half of the crew area was considered in poor condition. Slightly less than half of the unit was considered fair or marginally fair and remaining small portions of good habitat occurred in: the Turtle Mountains, the Devils Lake region, the extreme southeastern portion of stratum 46 in North Dakota, and in the northern reaches of the Prairie Coteau in South Dakota. Because of the general lack of water and the overall depressed wetland conditions, little if any second or late nesting was expected and below average waterfowl production was expected in the survey unit this year.

Northern Saskatchewan, Northern Manitoba, and Western Ontario: In northern Saskatchewan and northern Manitoba (strata 21-25), a very early spring break-up occurred. Winter snowfall was plentiful enough across both provinces to recharge most beaver ponds and small lakes. The early spring and good water conditions across the landscape should bode well for waterfowl production. Larger lakes and rivers tended to be higher than recent years. In Manitoba, the lakes associated with the Nelson River drainage were especially high and muddy. Floodwater extended well into the vegetation along the entire drainage. Along other major rivers, the flooding was prevalent, but not as severe. Although flooding could disrupt nesting on large water bodies, the early spring, coupled with ideal conditions on smaller wetlands, should produce good waterfowl production. Overall, the region was rated as good. In Western Ontario (stratum 50), spring was earlier than normal, lakes appeared full, and river flow was normal to high. Marsh habitat in Stratum 50 was also well flooded with adequate water levels. Waterfowl production throughout the survey area was expected to be good to excellent.

The total-duck estimate was 16% below the 2005 estimate, and 24% below the long-term average. All the major species estimates in this crew area were below long-term averages, except for green-winged teal, where numbers were unchanged from last year, and remained 54% above the long-term average. The scaup estimate was similar to last year's, and remained 43% lower than the long-term average. Mallards, gadwall, blue-winged teal and Northern pintail estimates were all similar to their 2005 estimates, but were 43%, 41%, 69%, and 86% below their long-term averages, respectively. American wigeon numbers were 40% below last year's estimate, and 58% below their long-term average for the region. Northern shovelers were 59% below last year's estimate, and 72% below their long-term average. Redhead (-61%) and canvasback (-67%) estimates declined relative to last year's, and were 82% and 77% below their long-term averages for the survey area.

As of July, conditions were rated mostly good, with some areas of fair, throughout most of northern Saskatchewan and Northern Manitoba.

Northern Alberta, Northeastern British Columbia, and Northwest Territories: Spring arrived two to three weeks earlier than normal 2006 to this survey area (strata 13-18, 20, 75-77), especially in northern Alberta and the southern Northwest Territories, and overall, breeding habitat was rated as good. The southern portion of Northern Alberta and Northeastern British Columbia (Stratum 77) bounded by Fort McMurray, Slave lake and the Peace River was dry because of below normal winter and spring precipitation. Conditions there were similar to, but not quite as dry as those of 2005. This area was rated fair. However, the northern portion of the stratum received more winter precipitation, and wetland conditions there were rated good. At survey time, all water bodies in Stratum 77 were ice free, which is highly unusual. Flooding on the Athabasca Delta (Stratum 20) was below normal, which decreased

available waterfowl breeding habitat. Most lake levels were low; only Lake Claire was near normal. Most water in the small wetlands and deeper sloughs was not expected to last into the summer, which likely adversely affected habitat for waterfowl broods. Although spring was 2-3 weeks early on the Delta, with no ice on Lake Claire, Stratum 20 was rated as fair due to low water levels. The southern Northwest Territories (Stratum 17) also experienced an early spring. Northern portions of the stratum were rated good, but flooding due to heavy May rains in the southern portion of the stratum meant conditions there were only fair. The Canadian Shield (Strata 16 and 18) was rated good, as water levels were near or above normal. Spring also began early in this region, but phenology was delayed in early and mid-May due to lower temperatures and snow. Conditions in the Middle Mackenzie Valley (Stratum 15) were good for waterfowl overall, due to above average snowmelt, despite a dry swath through the middle of this stratum. Spring phenology was slightly delayed in Stratum 14 (Upper Mackenzie Valley Boreal Plains/Tundra), but water levels were higher than normal, and overall conditions were good. Considerable flooding occurred on the Mackenzie River Delta (Stratum 13) but weather-related survey delays precluded more detailed reports on breeding conditions in this area.

Total-duck numbers were similar to the 2005 estimate, and 28% below the long-term average for the survey area. Green-winged teal numbers were 72% higher than their 2005 estimate and similar to their long-term average. Estimates of all other species were similar to those of 2005. Mallard (-49%), American wigeon (-38%), Northern pintail (-67%), and scaup (-55%) estimates were below their long-term averages for the survey area. By contrast, the gadwall estimate was 187% above the long-term average. All other species estimates for the area were similar to their long-term averages.

As of July, habitat conditions and the production outlook for this survey area remained unchanged since the survey was flown.

Alaska, Yukon Territory, and Old Crow Flats: In Alaska, the Yukon Territory, and Old Crow Flats (strata 1-12), breeding conditions depend largely on the timing of spring phenology, because wetland conditions are less variable than on the prairies. In general, Alaska experienced a later arrival of spring conditions than the early springs of recent years. Overall, a normal phenology occurred throughout Alaska and the Yukon

Territory. Ice lingered on the outer coast of the Yukon Delta, the northern Seward Penninsula, and on the Old Crow Flats. Some flooding occurred on the Koyukuk, the lower Innoko, and the lower Yukon Rivers. Overall, good waterfowl production is anticipated this year in the northwestern continental area, but cold weather in early June could reduce the outlook somewhat.

Estimates of all duck species were similar to those of 2005, with the exception of mallards, which were 27% below their 2005 count, but 44% above their long-term average, and Northern shovelers, which were 39% below their 2005 count, and 53% above their long-term average. Total duck (+34%), American wigeon (+61%), and green-winged teal (+118%) estimates were all above their long-term averages. This crew area was the only one in which the American wigeon estimate was above its long-term average. Blue-winged teal were 100% lower than their long-term average, but this survey area is not an important breeding area for this species. Gadwall, Northern pintail, redhead, canvasback, and scaup populations all remained similar to their long-term averages.

During June, weather in Alaska was variable. Coastal Alaska was colder and wetter than normal north of the Yukon River Delta, with normal temperatures and precipitation south of it. Interior Alaska experienced hard frosts, cold weather, and heavy precipitation that could lower brood survival Overall however, the forecast for production was unchanged, with good waterfowl production expected.

Eastern Survey Area: Spring-like conditions arrived early in most of the eastern U.S. and Canada (strata 51-72), with an early ice break-up and relatively mild temperatures. Biologists reported that habitat conditions were generally good across most of the survey area. Most regions had a warm, dry winter and a dry start to spring. Extreme southern Ontario was relatively dry during the survey period and habitats were in fair to poor condition. However, precipitation after survey completion improved habitat conditions in this region. Abundant rain in May improved water levels in Maine, the Maritimes, southern Ontario, and Quebec, but caused some flooding in southern Ontario and Quebec and along the coast of Maine, New Brunswick, and Nova Scotia. In Quebec, a very early spring assured good habitat availability. Despite the early spring and the abundance of spring precipitation, a dry winter still left most of the marshes and rivers drier than in past years. Many bogs were noticeably drier than

past years or dry entirely in a few cases. Winter precipitation increased to the west and north, resulting in generally good levels in central and northern Ontario. Conditions were good to excellent in central and northern Ontario due to the early spring phenology, generally good water levels, and warm spring temperatures.

Waterfowl habitat conditions in May, 2006 for the Atlantic crew area ranged from fair in the south to good in the north. Maine (stratum 62) and the Maritime provinces of Canada experienced a milder than normal winter with spring break-up occurring by late April. Phenology was at least two weeks advanced in all strata. Early in May, New Brunswick (stratum 63), Nova Scotia (stratum 64) and Prince Edward Island (stratum 65) were extremely dry as a result of limited snow pack run-off and little early spring rainfall. Temperatures were also above normal. Ponds and wetlands, however, were fully charged and adequate cover was available for early nesters. Southern portions of the survey area experienced heavy rainfall and flooding early in May and wet conditions continued throughout the month. This flooding could have affected some early nesters in parts of Maine, New Brunswick and Nova Scotia. Newfoundland (stratum 66) and Labrador (stratum 67) also had a milder than normal winter with little snow until late. Runoff was heavy in April, but by mid May streams and ponds were drier than normal. During the last week of May Newfoundland and Labrador received abundant rainfall and an end to the dry conditions. Phenology was at least two weeks early in Newfoundland and Labrador, but good nesting habitat was abundant and available for waterfowl.

Winter precipitation and temperatures were near long-term averages across much of southern Ontario and Quebec (Strata 52-59). Spring weather was mild, and precipitation was below normal this spring in southern Ontario prior to the survey. Extreme southern Ontario was relatively dry during the survey period and habitats were poor to fair. Wetland conditions improved near the Bruce Peninsula and south of the Georgian Bay with many seasonal wetlands in good condition. In the hardwood-boreal transition region east of Georgian Bay and into the agricultural regions of the Ottawa River Valley around Ottawa wetland conditions were also generally good. Generally favorable habitat conditions were observed throughout the St. Lawrence Lowlands of New York. Wetland habitats were in good condition in the St. Lawrence Lowlands in Ontario north through

Quebec City due to good winter and spring precipitation. Moderate flooding was observed during the survey east of Ottawa and in southeastern Quebec. Spring snow and ice-melt were uncharacteristically early in northern Ontario in the James Bay and Hudson Bay lowlands (Strata 57-59) for the second straight year. Heavy winter snowfall and a mild, early spring resulted in excellent prospects for waterfowl production. Waterfowl production throughout Central Ontario (Stratum 52) was expected to be good to excellent, due to an early spring phenology, generally good water levels, warm spring temperatures, and the resulting adequate brood cover. Habitat conditions in southern Quebec were drier than in recent years, but spring was early. A large hydroelectric project along the Eastmain River resulted in the loss of thousands of hectares of boreal forest and associated wetlands, and long-term effects are unclear. Habitat within the lower North Shore and Anticosti Island was considered good. Although marshes and rivers were drier than in recent years, waterfowl habitat was abundant. In boreal areas, an early spring is more important than good water levels so Quebec was rated good for waterfowl production overall in 2006.

Mergansers, mallards, American black ducks, ring-necked ducks, goldeneyes, scoters, scaup and green-winged teal were all similar to their 2005 estimates (Table 13). American wigeon (-51%) and buffleheads (-58%) were lower than their 2005 estimates. None of the species estimates in the eastern survey area differed from long-term averages. As of July, habitat conditions in the eastern survey area appeared unchanged since surveys were flown.

Other areas: Wetland conditions in many areas along the West Coast of the U.S. and Canada improved relative to the dry conditions that prevailed in 2005. In Oregon, total mallards in the breeding population were estimated at 88,000, similar to last year's count of 83,000, but 20% below the long-term average. The estimate for total ducks (263,000) was up 17% relative to 2005, but was 11% below the long-term average.

In British Columbia, snow packs were variable during the winter of 2005-06, good across southern regions, but below average in the central interior. Water levels in low elevation wetlands were higher than in 2005, but overall, remained poor. The total number of ducks observed in 2005 was similar to that of 2005, and to the (1988-2005) long-term average (LTA). Total diving ducks were 36% higher than in 2005 and 24% above the LTA.

Total dabbling duck counts were 51% higher than in 2005 and 8% above the LTA, but tests for statistical significance are not available for these counts. Mallard counts were down, but similar to those of 2005 and to the long-term average. These counts reflected both a dry spring and an overall improvement in wetland conditions relative to 2005 in central British Columbia. In California, winter precipitation was average, but spring weather brought precipitation totals to above average over most of the state. Excellent conditions prevailed in the northeastern part of the state where above normal production was expected. Elsewhere, duck nesting effort was late but strong and production was expected to be higher than normal. The total-duck estimate in 2006 was 649,400, which was similar to last year's estimate of 615,000, and the long-term average. The Mallard estimate in 2006 was 399,400, which was not significantly different from the 2005 estimate or the long-term average.

In Nebraska, habitat conditions in the Sandhills were initially good. Observers noted that duck numbers were similar to those in recent years. However, conditions deteriorated quickly as spring progressed and most temporary wetlands were dry by early June, and thus waterfowl production was expected to be only fair.

Waterfowl numbers were down in the Great Lakes states. In Minnesota, wetland conditions in spring 2006 were similar to those of 2005. Ice breakup on most lakes across the state occurred approximately 10 days earlier than average. April and May temperatures were above normal. Precipitation was above normal in April and below normal in May. Minnesota pond numbers decreased 12% relative to 2005, and were 15% below the 1968-2005 average. Mallard numbers continued to decline; the estimate of 161,000 was down 33% relative to the 2005 estimate of 238,500 and was 28% below the long-term average, but a test for statistical significance was unavailable for the latter. Total duck numbers, at 529,000, were also below their 2005 count. Spring precipitation was above average over much of Wisconsin, and wetland conditions were generally fair to good when breeding ducks arrived. Wetland numbers and conditions across the state were generally improved relative to 2005, but still below long term averages in many areas, which suggested average conditions overall. Heavy rains during the survey period and shortly thereafter likely improved brood habitat in many areas. The total duck estimate was 522,600 ± 51,500, and the mallard estimate was 219,500 ± 30,500. Wisconsin total duck numbers were 28% below the

29

2005 estimate and 22% above the 1974-2005 average. Mallard numbers were 31% below their 2005 level, and similar to the long-term mean. In Michigan, the mallard estimate of 208,000 was similar to that of 2005, and 50% below the 1992-2005 average

In the Atlantic Flyway states along the East Coast of the U.S., conditions early in the breeding season were generally favorable for nesting waterfowl, with warm temperatures and dry to normal moisture conditions. Heavy rains and cooler temperatures during May and June in the northern and western portions of the survey area may have affected production through nest flooding and brood losses. In the southern part of the survey area, cool temperatures and poor wetland conditions caused by less than normal precipitation provided poor conditions for brood rearing. Overall, field biologists' reports suggest that production this year may be reduced because of poor habitat and weather conditions. Total duck and mallard numbers from the Atlantic Flyway's Breeding Waterfowl survey were similar to 2005 estimates, and to their 1993-2005 averages.

Mallard Fall-flight Index

The mid-continent mallard population is composed of mallards from the traditional survey area, Michigan, Minnesota, and Wisconsin, and is 7.9 ± 0.2 million. This is similar to the 2005 estimate of 7.5 ± 0.3 million. The projected mallard fall flight index was 9.8 ± 0.1 million, similar to the 2005 estimate of 9.3 ± 0.1 million birds (Fig. 3). These indices were based on revised mid-continent mallard population models, and therefore, differ from those previously published (USFWS Adaptive Harvest Management Report 2005, Runge et al. 2002).

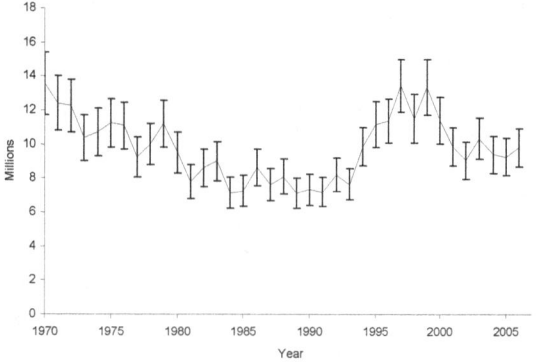

Fig. 5. Estimates and 90% confidence intervals for the size of the mallard population in the fall.

REFERENCES

Drought Watch on the Prairies, 2006. Agriculture and Agri-Food Canada. http://www.agr.gc.ca/pfra/main_e.html

Link, W. A., and J. R. Sauer. 2002. A hierarchical model of population change with application to Cerulean Warblers. Ecology 83:2832-2840.

NOAA/USDA Joint Agriculture Weather Facility. 2006. Weekly Weather and Crop Bulletin. Washington, DC. http://www.usda.gov/oce/weather/pubs/Weekly/Wwcb/index.htm

Runge, M. C., F. A. Johnson, J. A. Dubovsky, W. L. Kendall, J. Lawrence, J. Gammonley. 2002. A revised protocol for the Adaptive Harvest Management of Mid-Continent Mallards. (migratorybirds.fws.gov/reports/ahm02/MCMrevise2002.pdf)

Sauer, J.R., and S. Droege. 1990. Wood duck population trends from the North American Breeding Bird Survey. Pages 159-165 in L.H. Frederickson, G. V. Burger, S.P. Havera, D.A. Graber, R.E. Kirby, and T.S. Taylor, eds. Proceedings of the 1988 North American Wood Duck Symposium, St. Louis, MO.

U.S. Fish and Wildlife Service. 2006. Adaptive Harvest Management: 2006 Duck Hunting Season. U.S. Dept. Interior, Washington, D.C. U.S. Fish and Wildlife Service. 2006.

Waterfowl Breeding Population Surveys, 2006, Field Crew Reports. http://migratorybirds.fws.gov/reports/reports.html

Wilkins, K. A., M. C. Otto, and M. D. Koneff 2006. Trends in duck breeding populations, 1955-2006. U.S. Dept. Interior, Washington, D.C. 26pp. http://migratorybirds.fws.gov/reports/reports.html

STATUS OF GEESE AND SWANS

Abstract: We provide information on the population status and productivity of North American Canada geese (*Branta canadensis*), brant (*B. bernicla*), snow geese (*Chen caerulescens*), Ross' geese (*C. rossii*), emperor geese (*C. canagica*), white-fronted geese (*Anser albifrons*), and tundra swans *(Cygnus columbianus)*. In 2006, the timing of spring snowmelt in important goose and swan nesting areas in most of the Arctic and subarctic was earlier than average. Delayed nesting phenology or reduced nesting effort was indicated for only Alaska's Yukon Delta, other coastal areas of Alaska, and near the Mackenzie River Delta in the western Canadian Arctic. Primary abundance indices in 2006 increased from 2005 levels for 13 goose populations and decreased for 11 goose populations. Primary abundance indices in 2006 for both populations of tundra swans increased from 2005 levels. The Mississippi Flyway Giant and the Atlantic Canada goose populations, the Western Arctic/Wrangel Island snow goose population, and Pacific white-fronted goose population displayed significant positive trends during the most recent 10-year period (*P* < 0.05). The Short Grass Prairie Canada goose and the Mid-continent light goose populations showed significant negative 10-year trends. The forecast for the production of geese and swans in North America in 2006 is generally favorable and improved from that of 2005.

This section summarizes information regarding the status, annual production of young, and expected fall flights of goose and tundra swan populations in North America. Information was compiled from a broad geographic area and is provided to assist managers in regulating harvest.

Most populations of geese and swans in North America nest in the Arctic or subarctic regions of Alaska and northern Canada (Fig. 1), but several Canada goose populations nest in temperate regions of the United States and southern Canada ("temperate-nesting" populations). The annual production of young by northern-nesting geese is influenced greatly by weather conditions on the breeding grounds, especially the timing of spring snowmelt and its impact on the initiation of nesting activity (i.e., phenology). Persistent snow cover reduces nest site availability, delays nesting activity, and often results in depressed reproductive effort and productivity. In general, goose productivity will be better than average if nesting begins by late May in western and central portions of the Arctic, and by early June in the eastern Arctic. Production usually is poor if nest initiations are delayed much beyond 15 June. For temperate-nesting Canada goose populations, recruitment rates are less variable, but productivity is influenced by localized drought and flood events.

METHODS

We have used the most widely accepted nomenclature for various waterfowl populations, but they may differ from other published information. Species nomenclature follows the List of Migratory Birds in Title 50 of the Code of Federal Regulations, Section 10.13. Some of the goose populations described herein are comprised of more than 1 subspecies and some light goose populations contain 2 species (i.e., snow and Ross' geese).

Population estimates for geese are derived from a variety of surveys conducted by biologists from federal, state, and provincial agencies, and universities (Appendices B, I, and J). Surveys include the Midwinter Survey (MWS, conducted each January in wintering areas), the Waterfowl Breeding Population and Habitat Survey (WBPHS, see Duck section of this report), surveys that are specifically designed for various populations, and others. When survey methodology allowed, 95% confidence intervals were presented with population estimates. The 10-year trends of population estimates were calculated through regression of the natural logarithm of survey results on year, and slope coefficients were presented and tested for equality to zero (*t*-test). Changes in population indices between the current and previous years were calculated and, where possible, assessed with a *z*-test using the sum of sampling variances for the 2 estimates. Primary abundance indices, those related to management plan population objectives, are described first in population-specific sections and graphed when data are available.

Because this report was completed prior to the final annual assessment of goose and swan reproduction, the annual productivity of most populations is only predicted qualitatively. Information on habitat conditions and forecasts of productivity were based primarily on observations made during various waterfowl surveys and on interviews with field biologists. These reports provide reliable information for specific locations, but may not provide accurate assessment for the vast geographic range of waterfowl populations.

Fig. 1. Important goose nesting areas in Arctic and subarctic North America.

RESULTS AND DISCUSSION

Conditions in the Arctic and Subarctic

The timing of spring snowmelt in nearly all important northern goose and swan nesting areas in 2006 was earlier than average. Many areas reported lower than average winter snow accumulation and higher than average temperatures during April-June 2006. Delayed nesting phenology or reduced nesting effort was indicated for only Alaska's Yukon Delta, other portions of western Alaska, and near the Mackenzie River Delta in the western Canadian Arctic. The snow and ice cover graphic (Fig. 2, National Oceanic and Atmospheric Administration) illustrates many similarities in the progression of snowmelt by 2 June in 2006 and 2005. Nesting phenology during 2005 was also widely reported as earlier than average.

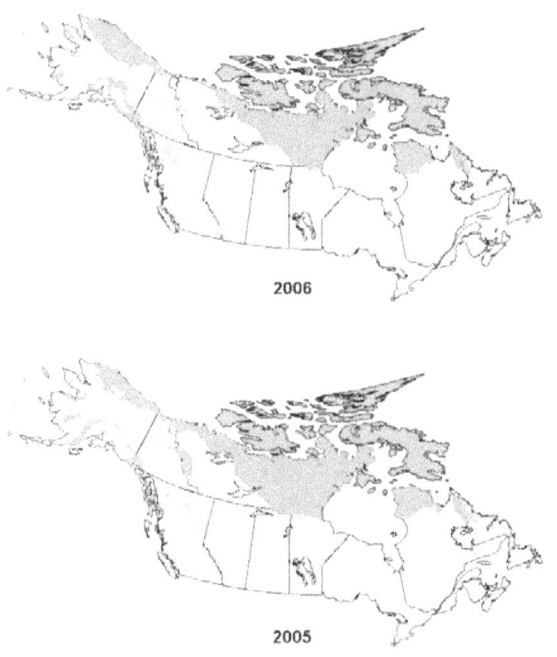

Fig. 2. The extent of snow and ice cover in North America on 2 June 2006 and 2 June 2005 (data from National Oceanic and Atmospheric Administration).

Conditions in Southern Canada and the United States

Conditions that influence the productivity of Canada geese vary less from year to year in these temperate regions than in the Arctic and subarctic. Given adequate wetland numbers and the absence of flood events, temperate-nesting Canada geese are reliably productive. Wetland abundance increased in many prairie and deciduous forest areas in 2006 and may benefit nesting geese. However, widespread spring flooding reduced goose production in some areas (e.g., New England, Utah). Drought impacted fewer areas in 2006 than in 2005, but still depressed production in some locales (e.g., western Oklahoma). Most temperate-nesting Canada goose populations likely experienced average or above average nesting conditions in 2006.

Status of Canada Geese

North Atlantic Population (NAP): NAP Canada geese principally nest in Newfoundland and Labrador. They generally commingle during winter with other Atlantic Flyway Canada geese, although NAP geese have a more coastal distribution than other populations (Fig. 3).

During the 2006 WBPHS, biologists estimated 49,200 ($\pm$ 24,800) indicated pairs (singles plus pairs) within NAP range (strata 66 and 67), 4% fewer than in 2005 ($P = 0.903$, Fig. 4). Indicated pair estimates have declined an average of 3% per year during 1997-2006 ($P = 0.228$). The 2006 estimate of 118,000 ($\pm$ 57,600) total NAP Canada geese was 9% lower than last year's estimate ($P = 0.784$). Preliminary information from the 2006 expanded CWS helicopter plot surveys indicated that numbers of geese increased from 2005 levels and that clutch sizes were again high. Spring phenology was nearly 2 weeks early and nesting conditions were favorable for geese in Newfoundland and Labrador in 2006. A fall flight similar to that of 2005 is expected.

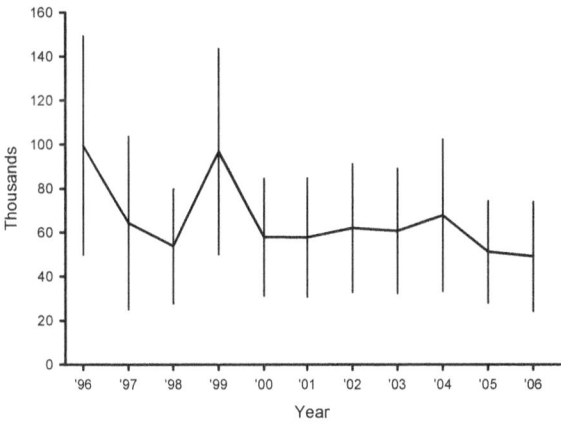

Fig. 4. Estimated number (and 95% confidence intervals) of North Atlantic Population Canada geese breeding pairs during spring.

33

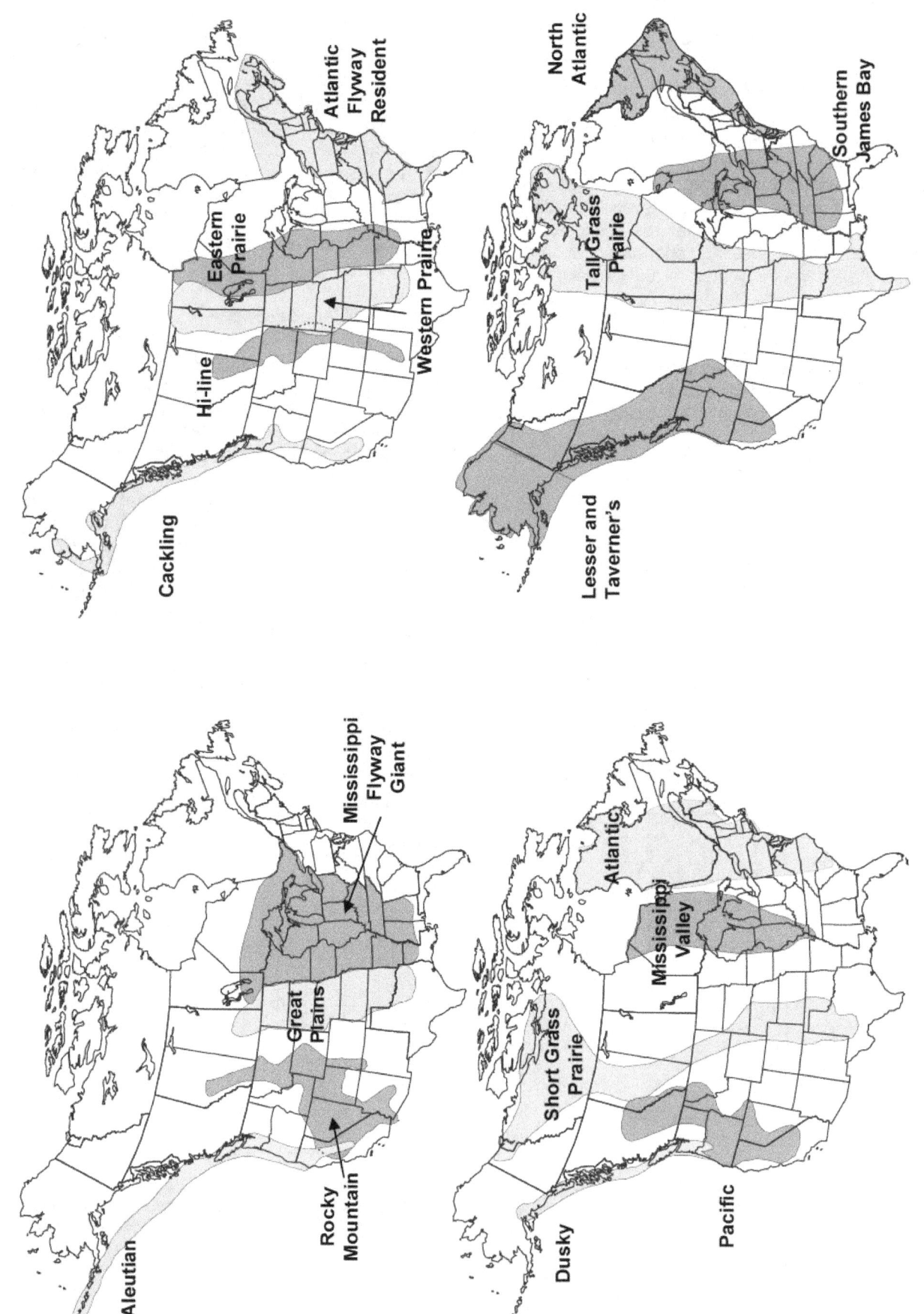

Fig. 3. Approximate ranges of Canada goose populations in North America.

34

Atlantic Population (AP): AP Canada geese nest throughout much of Quebec, especially along Ungava Bay, the eastern shore of Hudson Bay, and on the Ungava Peninsula. The AP winters from New England to South Carolina, but the largest concentrations occur on the Delmarva Peninsula (Fig. 3).

Spring surveys in 2006 yielded an estimate of 160,000 (± 32,200) indicated breeding pairs, 1% fewer than in 2005 ($P = 0.909$, Fig. 5). Breeding pair estimates have increased an average of 14% per year during 1997-2006 ($P < 0.001$). The estimated total spring population of 1,135,500 (± 237,700) geese in 2006 was nearly identical to that of last year ($P = 0.973$). Spring temperatures in 2006 were mild and breeding areas were largely free of snow by early May, leading to a second consecutive year of earlier than average nesting phenology in much of the AP range. The proportion of indicated pairs observed as singles (62%) surpassed the 2005 record-high level, suggesting another excellent nesting effort this year. Clutch sizes and nest densities on the Ungava Peninsula study areas in 2006 were slightly above average, and productivity there was expected to be average or better. Range-wide production was expected to be good and a fall flight similar to that of last year is expected.

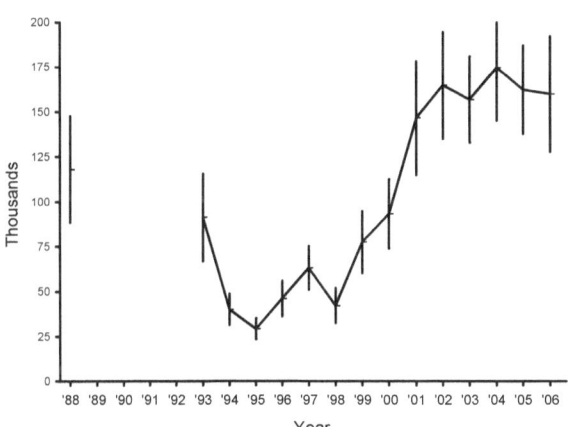

Fig. 5. Estimated number (and 95% confidence intervals) of Atlantic Population Canada goose breeding pairs in northern Quebec.

Atlantic Flyway Resident Population (AFRP): This population of large Canada geese inhabits southern Quebec, the southern Maritime provinces, and all states of the Atlantic Flyway (Fig. 3).

In 2003, the calculation method of the spring AFRP index was changed (survey methodology did not change). Beginning this year we discuss the new indices of the AFRP, but include the old indices graphically (Fig. 6). Surveys during spring 2006 estimated 1,149,100 (± 208,900) Canada geese in

this population, 2% fewer than in 2005 (1,167,100, $P = 0.903$). These indices have increased an average of 2% per year over the last 4 years ($P = 0.547$). Spring conditions in 2006 were near average in much of AFRP range. However, widespread flooding in the northeastern United States negatively impacted nesting there. Observations during banding programs in those areas indicated gosling production may have been reduced about 25% from average levels. The 2006 fall flight is expected to be somewhat less than average.

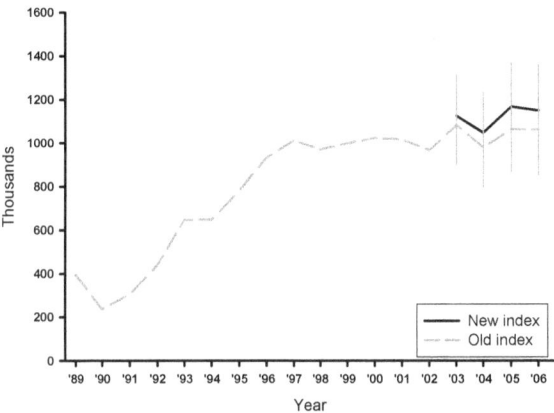

Fig. 6. Estimated number (and 95% confidence intervals) of Atlantic Flyway Resident Population Canada geese during spring.

Southern James Bay Population (SJBP): This population nests on Akimiski Island and in the Hudson Bay Lowlands to the west and south of James Bay. The SJBP winters from southern Ontario and Michigan to Mississippi, Alabama, Georgia, and South Carolina (Fig. 3).

Breeding ground surveys indicated a spring population of 160,400 (± 35,700) Canada geese in 2006, 247% higher than last year's potentially biased survey ($P < 0.001$), and 59% higher than the 2004 survey estimate ($P = 0.24$, Fig. 7). The 2006 level was a record high since surveys started in 1990. Spring population estimates have decreased an average of 2% per year since 1997 ($P = 0.646$). The estimate of breeding pairs in 2006 increased to 64,400 (± 13,900), 205% higher than in 2005 ($P < 0.001$), and 71% higher than in 2004 ($P = 0.075$). Biologists believed the 2005 survey results underestimated the population due to unusual variation in survey timing and reduced goose detection resulting from the use of a different survey aircraft. Surveys in 2006 were conducted within the target period with the traditionally used aircraft. Survey biologists indicated that temperate-nesting molt migrants likely were not a factor in survey estimates during 2004-2006. Lower than average winter snowfall and above average spring temperatures contributed to a spring thaw in 2006 that was even earlier than in 2005, and 3-4 weeks earlier than average. On Akimiski Island, nesting phenology was similar to 2005, which was the earliest recorded since 1993. Nest density and average clutch size on Akimiski Island were above the recent average. Nest success there was lower than in 2005, but still higher than average. Biologists anticipate the fall flight in 2006 to be well above average.

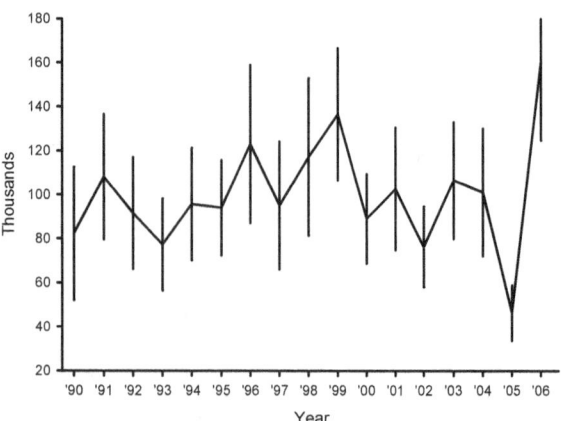

Fig. 7. Estimated total population (and 95% confidence intervals) of Southern James Bay Population Canada geese during spring.

Mississippi Valley Population (MVP): The principal nesting range of this population is in northern Ontario, especially in the Hudson Bay Lowlands, west of Hudson and James Bays. MVP Canada geese primarily concentrate during fall and winter in Wisconsin, Illinois, and Michigan (Fig. 3).

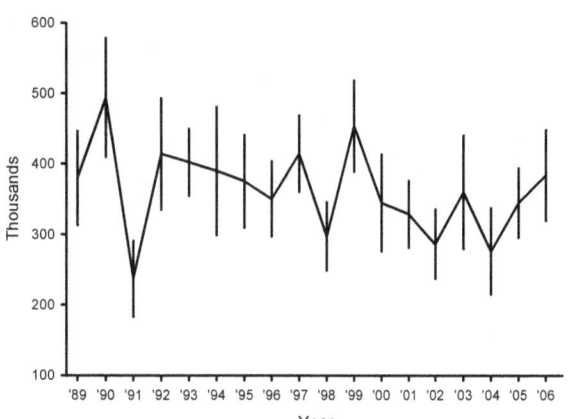

Fig. 8. Estimated number (and 95% confidence intervals) of Mississippi Valley Population breeding Canada geese during spring.

Breeding ground surveys conducted in 2006 indicated the presence of 384,400 ($\pm$ 64,100) MVP breeding adults, 11% more than in 2005 ($P = 0.339$),

and the highest number recorded since 1999. Estimates of breeding adults have declined an average of 1% per year during 1997-2006 ($P = 0.495$). Surveys indicated a total population of 705,000 ($\pm$ 138,000) Canada geese, a 31% increase from 2005 ($P = 0.061$, Fig. 8). Molt migrant Canada geese likely had little impact on the total goose estimate this year. For the second consecutive year, spring snowmelt occurred nearly a month earlier than in 2004 and much earlier than average. Residents of Peawanuck, Ontario reported the earliest break-up of the Winisk River within memory. Favorable spring conditions and higher than average nest densities suggest the 2006 fall flight should be similar to that of 2005.

Eastern Prairie Population (EPP): These geese nest in the Hudson Bay Lowlands of Manitoba and concentrate primarily in Manitoba, Minnesota, and Missouri during winter (Fig. 3).

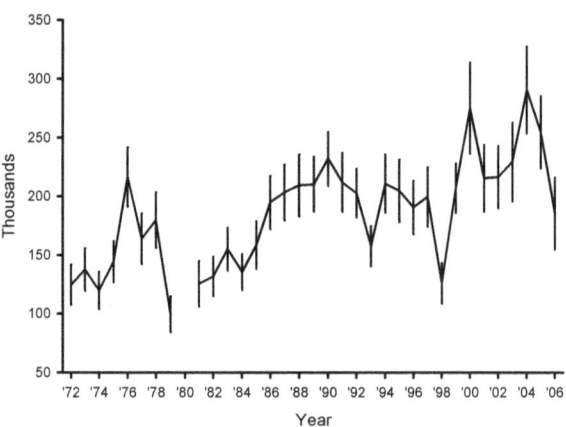

Fig. 9. Estimated number (and 95% confidence intervals) of Eastern Prairie Population Canada geese during spring.

The 2006 spring estimate of EPP geese was 185,400 ($\pm$ 30,400), 27% lower than the 2005 estimate ($P = 0.002$, Fig. 9). Spring estimates have increased an average of 3% per year over the last 10 years ($P = 0.222$). The 2006 survey estimate of singles and pairs was 134,800 ($\pm$ 18,700), 17% lower than last year ($P = 0.063$). Estimates of these population components have increased an average of 2% per year during 1997-2006 ($P = 0.113$). The estimated number of productive geese in 2006 was similar to 2005. Mild April temperatures and low winter snowfall led to an early nesting chronology throughout EPP range. This year, biologists on Cape Churchill observed a median hatch date of 17 June, about 1 week earlier than the long-term average (1976-2005). Nest density in 2006 was the highest recorded since 1990 and mean clutch size (4.1) was above the long-term average. Estimates of nest

36

density, clutch size, and nest success indicated production would be better than most recent years, but still slightly below the average value since 1976. Canada goose nest density, clutch size, and nest success indices compiled at the Broad River also indicated good production in 2006. A fall flight similar to that of 2005 is expected.

Mississippi Flyway Giant Population (MFGP): Giant Canada geese have been reestablished or introduced in all Mississippi Flyway states. This subspecies now represents a large proportion of all Canada geese in the Mississippi Flyway (Fig. 3).

During spring 2006 biologists tallied 1,686,300 MFGP geese, a record high, and 7% more than were tallied in 2005 (Fig. 10). These estimates have increased an average of 5% per year since 1997 ($P < 0.001$). Most MFGP states expected average production in 2006, with especially good nesting conditions in Iowa, Indiana, and Michigan. A large fall flight, similar to that of 2005 is expected.

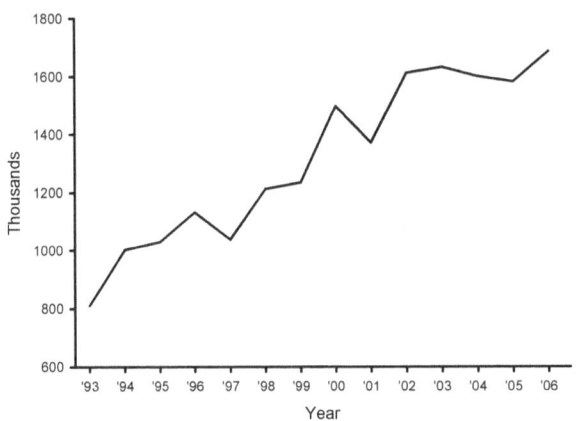

Fig. 10. Estimated number of Mississippi Flyway Giant Population Canada geese during spring.

Western Prairie and Great Plains Populations (WPP/GPP): The WPP is composed of mid-sized and large Canada geese that nest in eastern Saskatchewan and western Manitoba. The GPP is composed of large Canada geese resulting from restoration efforts in Saskatchewan, North Dakota, South Dakota, Nebraska, Kansas, Oklahoma, and Texas. Geese from these breeding populations commingle during migration with other Canada geese along the Missouri River in the Dakotas and on reservoirs from southwestern Kansas to Texas (Fig. 3). These 2 populations are managed jointly and surveyed during winter.

During the 2006 MWS, 444,400 WPP/GPP geese were counted, 7% more than in 2005 (Fig. 11). These indices have shown no trend during 1997-2006 ($P = 0.986$). In 2006, the estimated spring

population in the portion of WPP/GPP range included in the WBPHS was 733,200 ($\pm$ 116,000) geese, 24% more than last year ($P = 0.056$). The WBPHS estimates have increased an average of 4% per year since 1997 ($P = 0.005$). Goose production in the WPP range likely increased from 2005 due to slightly improved wetland conditions. Most states throughout GPP range reported near average nesting conditions and production. However, production in central North Dakota and in central and western Oklahoma was likely reduced by drought. A spring snow storm in Nebraska may have negatively impacted some geese there, but production was still expected to be average or above average. A fall flight similar to that of last year is expected.

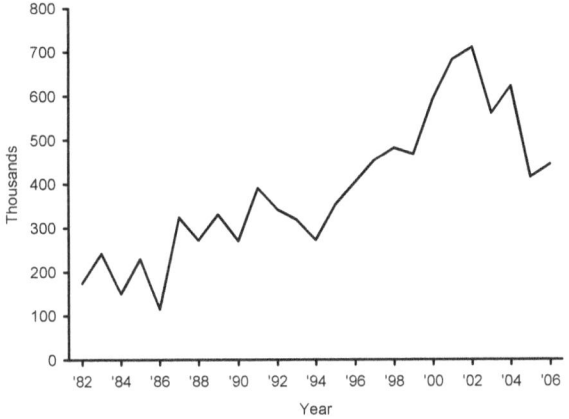

Fig. 11. Estimated number of Western Prairie Population/Great Plains Population Canada geese during winter.

Tall Grass Prairie Population (TGPP): These small Canada geese nest on Baffin (particularly on the Great Plain of the Koukdjuak), Southampton, and King William Islands; north of the Maguse and McConnell Rivers on the Hudson Bay coast; and in the eastern Queen Maud Gulf region. TGPP Canada geese winter mainly in Oklahoma, Texas, and northeastern Mexico (Fig. 3). These geese mix with other Canada geese on wintering areas, making it difficult to estimate the size of the winter population.

During the 2006 MWS in the Central Flyway, 499,800 TGPP geese were counted, 25% more than in 2005 (Fig. 12). These estimates have increased an average of 6% per year during 1997-2006 ($P = 0.236$). Average spring temperatures throughout western and southern Nunavut reached record highs in 2006. Biologists report that the timing of snowmelt and nesting activities in 2006 were earlier than recent years in the Queen Maud Gulf Sanctuary and on Southampton and King William Islands, but near average at the McConnell River. Satellite imagery and climate data suggest that Baffin Island snowmelt was earlier than in 2005. Limited information suggests production of TGPP Canada geese will be increased from that of 2005.

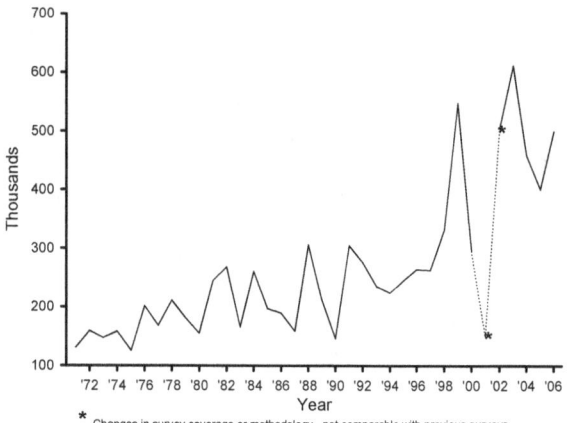

Fig. 12. Estimated number of Tall Grass Prairie Population Canada geese in the Central Flyway during winter.

*Changes in survey coverage or methodology - not comparable with previous surveys

Short Grass Prairie Population (SGPP): These small Canada geese nest on Victoria and Jenny Lind Islands and on the mainland from the Queen Maud Gulf west and south to the Mackenzie River and northern Alberta. These geese winter in southeastern Colorado, northeastern New Mexico, and the Oklahoma and Texas panhandles (Fig. 3).

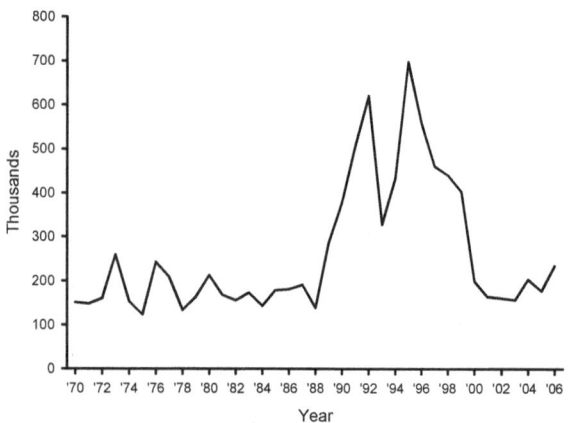

Fig. 13. Estimated number of Short Grass Prairie Population Canada geese during winter.

The MWS index of SGPP Canada geese in 2006 was 234,700, 33% higher than in 2005 (Fig. 13). These indices have declined an average of 10% per year since 1997 ($P = 0.024$). In 2006, the estimated spring population of SGPP geese in the Northwest Territories (WBPHS strata 13-18) was 87,500 ($\pm$ 33,500), a 25% decrease from 2005 ($P = 0.326$). WBPHS estimates have increased an average of 5% per year since 1997 ($P = 0.159$). Spring break-up was nearly a month earlier than average near Kugluktuk (west of Queen Maud Gulf), and the

average spring temperatures throughout western Nunavut reached record highs in 2006. Goose nesting phenology near Queen Maud Gulf in 2006 was about a week earlier than average. Snowmelt on Victoria Island also was earlier than average. Surveys near the Mackenzie Delta suggested a modest nesting effort by Canada geese there. Wetland conditions in WBPHS strata 13-18 were considered favorable for waterfowl nesting. Although specific information is limited, production from SGPP geese is expected to be higher than average in 2006.

Hi-line Population (HLP): These large Canada geese nest in southeastern Alberta, southwestern Saskatchewan, eastern Montana and Wyoming, and in Colorado. They winter in these states and central New Mexico (Fig. 3).

The 2006 MWS indicated a total of 247,300 HLP Canada geese, 19% more than last year's estimate (Fig. 14). The MWS estimates have increased an average of 4% per year since 1997 ($P = 0.119$). The WBPHS yields an estimate of the HLP spring population in Saskatchewan, Alberta, and Montana. The 2006 WBPHS estimate was 208,000 ($\pm$ 43,600), 12% lower than the 2005 estimate ($P = 0.401$). The WBPHS population estimates have shown no annual trend during 1997-2006 ($P = 0.723$). The state estimate of the HLP breeding population in Wyoming was 19,000, an increase of 3% from 2005. Wetland conditions were good to excellent in the northern portion of HLP range, but average to poor in southern areas. The fall flight of HLP geese is expected to be similar to that of 2005.

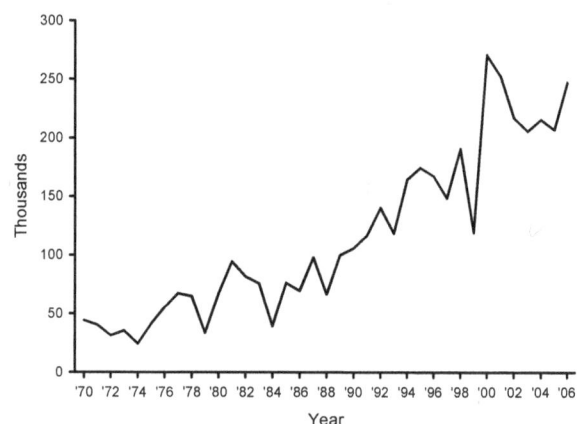

Fig. 14. Estimated number of Hi-line Population Canada geese during winter.

Rocky Mountain Population (RMP): These large Canada geese nest in southern Alberta and western Montana, and the inter-mountain regions of Utah, Idaho, Nevada, Wyoming, and Colorado. They winter mainly in central and southern California,

Arizona, Nevada, Utah, Idaho, and Montana (Fig. 3).

Spring population estimates from RMP states and provinces in 2006 totaled 140,600, 19% lower than in 2005 (Fig. 15). These estimates have increased an average of 3% per year during the last 10 years ($P = 0.186$). Population indices in 2006 increased in Wyoming, Colorado, and Nevada, but decreased in Alberta, Montana, and Utah. Wetland conditions in Alberta and Montana improved since 2005 which may increase goose production there. Utah experienced widespread spring flooding and biologists there expected gosling production to be reduced. The fall flight of RMP geese is expected to be similar to that of last year.

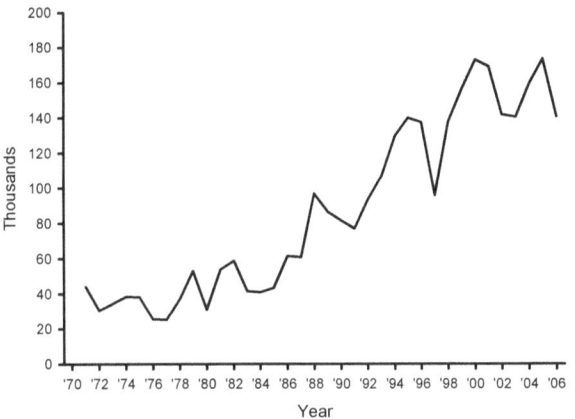

Fig. 15. Estimated number of Rocky Mountain Population Canada geese during spring.

Pacific Population (PP): These large Canada geese nest and winter west of the Rocky Mountains from northern Alberta and British Columbia south through the Pacific Northwest to California (Fig. 3).

Most PP geese are surveyed in Alberta and Oregon. In 2006, survey indices in Alberta (WBPHS strata 76-77) and Oregon were 73,200 ($\pm$ 43,400) and 41,900, respectively. These indices represent an increase of 65% ($P = 0.255$) and no change, respectively, from indices in 2005. Breeding population indices in 2006 also increased from the 2005 levels in British Columbia and Washington, but decreased in California and Nevada. Habitat conditions were favorable in northern Alberta. California and Utah expected gosling production in 2006 to be below average due to spring storms or flooding events. Wetland conditions in Nevada and the production outlook there have improved since 2005. A fall flight similar to that of 2005 is expected.

Dusky Canada Geese: These mid-sized Canada geese predominantly nest on the Copper River Delta of southeastern Alaska, and winter principally in the Willamette and Lower Columbia River Valleys of Oregon and Washington (Fig. 3).

The size of the population is estimated through observations of marked geese during December and January. The 2005-2006 population estimate was 11,900 ($\pm$ 2,200), 45% lower than in 2004-2005 ($P < 0.001$, Fig. 16). These estimates have decreased an average of 1% per year during the last 10-year period ($P = 0.763$). Preliminary results from the 2006 spring survey of Copper River Delta dusky geese indicated the index of singles and pairs decreased 25%, and total geese decreased 34% from last year's high levels. Although lower than in 2005, the 2006 breeding ground indices exceeded levels recorded in all other years since 1998. In 2006, the Copper River Delta experienced a cold spring, resulting in snowmelt and nesting phenology being somewhat later than average (by less than 1 week). Nest success was lower than average in 2006 based on predation rates observed at artificial nest islands. A fall flight somewhat lower than that of last year is expected.

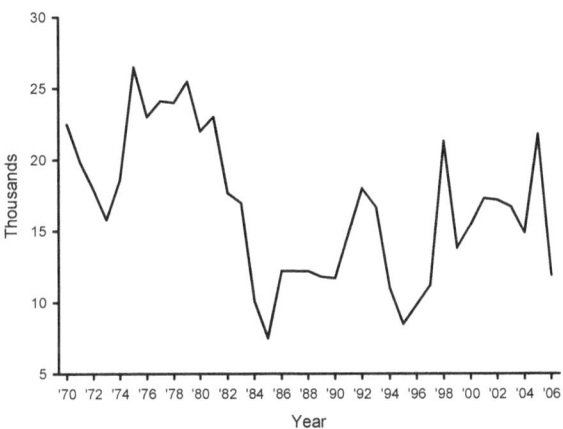

Fig. 16. Estimated number of dusky Canada geese during winter.

Cackling Canada Geese: Cackling Canada geese nest on the Yukon-Kuskokwim Delta (YKD) of western Alaska. They primarily winter in the Willamette and Lower Columbia River Valleys of Oregon and Washington (Fig. 3).

The primary index of this population was a fall estimate from 1979-1998. Since 1999, the index has been an estimate of the subsequent fall population derived from spring counts of adults on the YKD. The fall estimate for 2006 is 169,300, 8% higher than that of 2005. These estimates have decreased an average of 2% per year since 1997 ($P = 0.246$, Fig. 17). Surveys in the coastal zone of the YKD during spring 2006 indicated increases of 10% and 8% in the numbers of indicated pairs and total geese, respectively, from 2005 estimates. Spring snowmelt on the YKD was about 1 week later than average, but goose nesting phenology was only 2-3 days later than the long-term average. Yukon Delta nesting surveys indicated that clutch sizes in 2006 were near the 1997-2005 average. Fox predation appeared to be low in 2006 and nest success rates should be high. A fall flight similar to that of last year is expected.

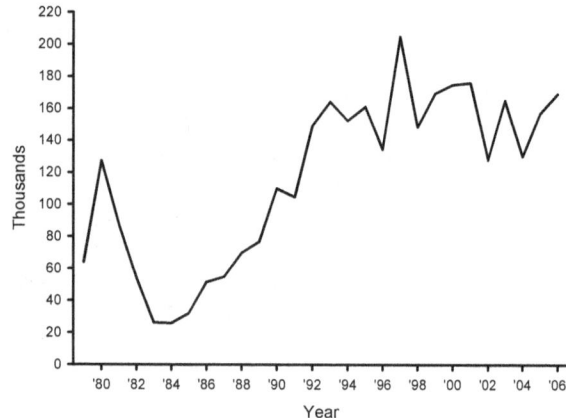

Fig. 17. Number of cackling Canada geese estimated from fall and spring surveys.

Lesser and Taverner's Canada Geese: These subspecies nest throughout much of interior and south-central Alaska and winter in Washington, Oregon, and California (Fig. 3). Taverner's geese are more associated with the North Slope and tundra areas, while lesser Canada geese tend to nest in Alaska's interior. However, these subspecies mix with other Canada geese throughout the year and reliable estimates of separate populations are not presently available.

The 2006 estimate of Canada geese within WBPHS strata predominantly occupied by these subspecies (strata 1-6, 8, 10-12) was 61,300, nearly identical to the 2005 estimate (61,000). These estimates have declined an average of 5% per year since 1997 (P = 0.012). In Alaska's interior, spring break-up varied from near average to 1 week later than average. Substantial flooding was limited to the Koyukuk area. Production of lesser Canada geese in the interior is expected to be good or very good. Spring snowmelt on the North Slope was 5-7 days earlier than average and goose production of Taverner's geese there is expected to be good.

Aleutian Canada Geese (ACG): The Aleutian Canada goose was listed as endangered in 1967 (the population numbered approximately 800 birds in 1974) and was de-listed in 2001. These geese now nest primarily on the Aleutian Islands, although historically they nested from near Kodiak Island,

Alaska to the Kuril Islands in Asia. They now winter along the Pacific Coast to central California (Fig. 3).

The population estimate for these geese has been based on observations of neck-banded geese in California. At the time this report was prepared the 2005-2006 population estimate was not available. During 2004-2005, the population estimate was 63,800 ($\pm$ 12,400), 9% lower than the record high estimate in 2003-2004 (P = 0.555, Fig. 18). Those indirect estimates had increased an average of 12% per year during winters of 1995 through 2005 (P < 0.001). In 2006, the Aleutian Islands experienced a late spring snowmelt and nesting phenology of Aleutian Canada geese was somewhat delayed. However, clutch sizes were near average and reports from Buldir Island indicate production was average or better there. Production in 2006 may be near average but likely will be reduced from the 2 previous years.

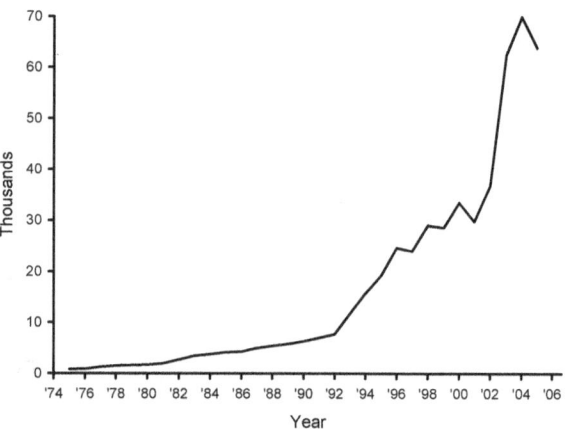

Fig. 18. Number of Aleutian Canada geese estimated from winter estimates and mark-resight methods.

Status of Light Geese

The term light geese refers to both snow geese and Ross' geese (including both white and blue color phases), and the lesser (*C. c. caerulescens*) and greater (*C. c. atlantica*) snow goose subspecies. Another collective term, mid-continent light geese, includes lesser snow and Ross' geese of 2 populations: the Mid-continent Population and the Western Central Flyway Population.

Ross' Geese: Most Ross' geese nest in the Queen Maud Gulf region, but increasing numbers nest along the western coast of Hudson Bay, and Southampton, Baffin, and Banks Islands. Ross' geese are present in the range of 3 different populations of light geese and primarily winter in California, New Mexico,

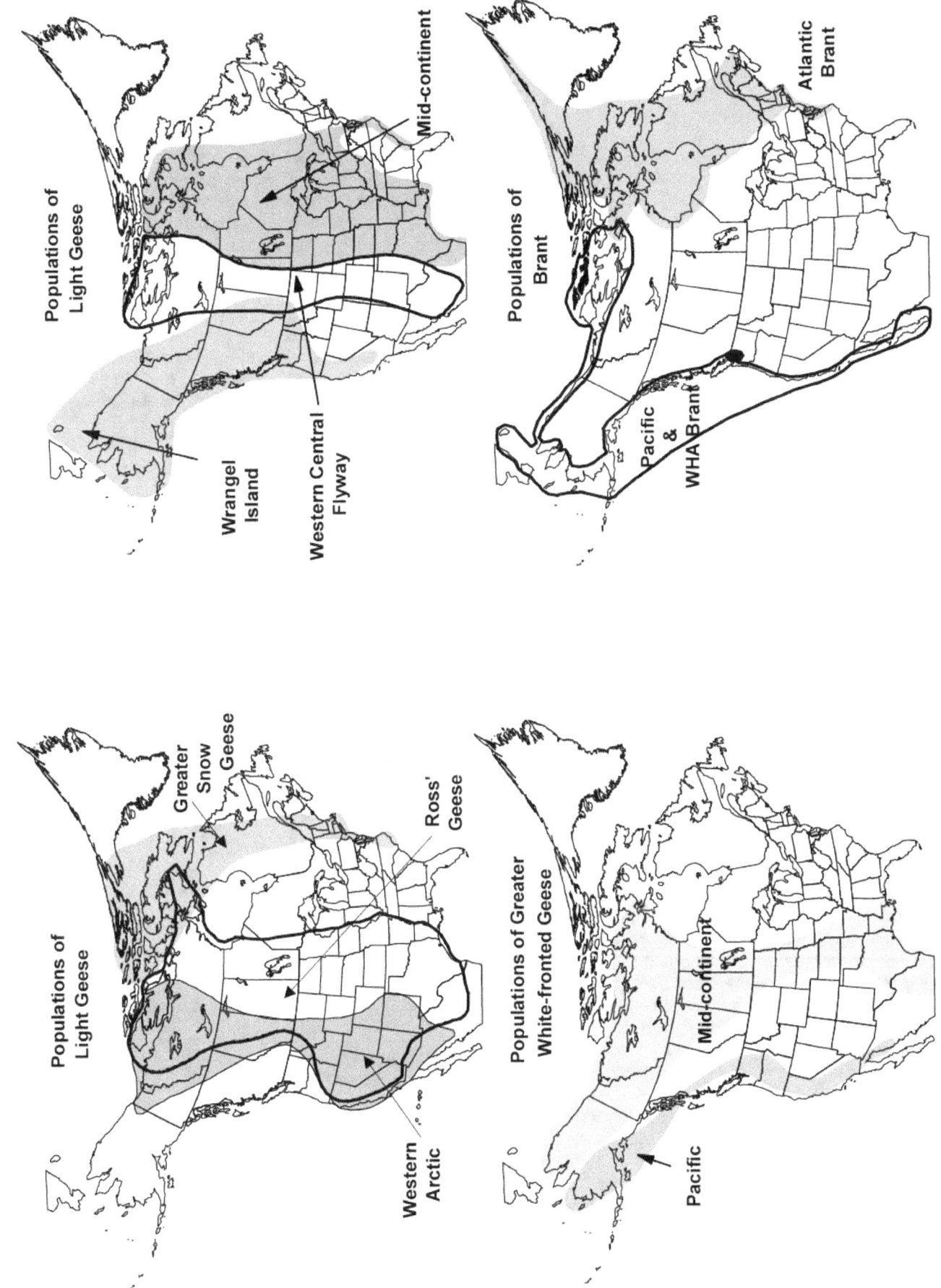

Fig. 19. Approximate ranges of brant and snow, Ross', and white-fronted goose populations in North America.

41

Texas, and Mexico, with increasing numbers in Louisiana and Arkansas (Fig. 19).

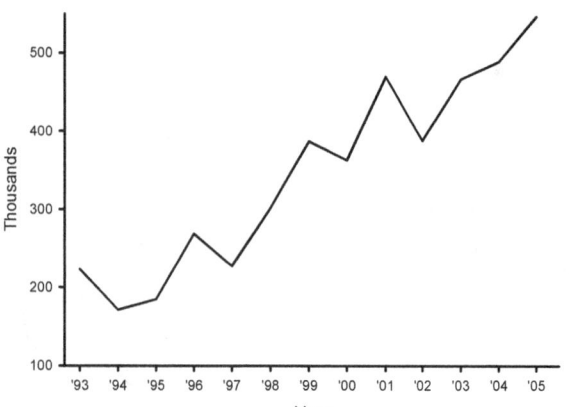

Fig. 20. Estimated number adult Ross' geese nesting at the Karrak Lake colony, Nunavut.

Ross' geese are annually surveyed at only 2 of their numerous nesting colonies. More comprehensive aerial photography inventories and groundwork (to identify proportions of snow and Ross' geese within colonies) are conducted only periodically. The largest Ross' goose colonies are in the Queen Maud Gulf Sanctuary. Biologists there estimated that 546,700 adult Ross's geese nested at the Karrak Lake colony in 2005, a 12% increase from 2004 (Fig. 20). These estimates have increased an average of 11% during 1996-2005. Although population estimates for 2006 are not yet available, the area of the Karrak Lake colony grew to 215 km^2 this year, 8% larger than in 2005. Colony 10, about 60 miles to the east of Karrak Lake has grown to contain similar or higher numbers of Ross' geese, and in 2006 held very high nest densities. Spring break-up was nearly a month earlier than average near Kugluktuk (west of Queen Maud Gulf), and average spring temperatures throughout western Nunavut reached record highs in 2006. Nesting phenology at Queen Maud Gulf was about 1 week earlier than average and gosling production is expected to be above average. At the McConnell River colony on the west coast of Hudson Bay in 2006, biologists estimated the presence of 85,600 (± 16,500) nesting light geese, of which about 95% are Ross' geese. The 2006 McConnell colony estimate was about 10% lower than the 2005 estimate and similar to that of 2004. Nesting phenology at the McConnell River appeared to be average or earlier, although local residents reported a colder than average spring. Mean clutch size was 3.3 and predation appeared to be low in 2006. Ross' geese are also abundant on Southampton Island where

spring snowmelt and goose nesting phenology was reportedly earlier than average. Overall, Ross' geese are expected to experience better than average production this year.

Mid-continent Population Light Geese (MCP): This population includes lesser snow geese and increasing numbers of Ross' geese. Geese of the MCP nest on Baffin and Southampton Islands, with smaller numbers nesting along the west coast of Hudson Bay (Fig. 19). These geese winter primarily in eastern Texas, Louisiana, and Arkansas.

During the 2006 MWS, biologists counted 2,221,700 light geese, 5% fewer than last year (Fig. 21). Winter indices during 1997-2006 indicate an average population decline of 3% per year (P = 0.005). Climate records from Cape Dorset and Iqaluit on Baffin Island, and from Coral Harbour on Southampton Island indicate that April, May, and June of 2006 were all 1-4°C warmer than the long-term averages. Accordingly, satellite imagery suggests Baffin Island snowmelt was earlier in 2006 than in 2005. Biologists on Southampton Island reported that spring snowmelt was about 1 week earlier than recent years. Nesting phenology there appeared to be 3-4 days earlier than in 2005 and 2 weeks earlier than in 2004. Spring phenology at Cape Henrietta Maria and La Perouse Bay was earlier than average for a second consecutive year and biologists expect production there to be average or better. A fall flight similar to or larger than that of 2005 is expected.

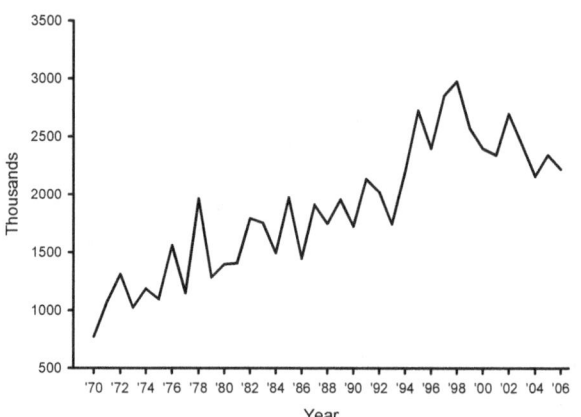

Fig. 21. Estimated number of Mid-continent Population light geese (lesser snow and Ross' geese) during winter.

Western Central Flyway Population (WCFP): This population is composed primarily of snow geese, but includes a substantial proportion of Ross' geese. Geese of the WCFP nest in the central and western Canadian Arctic, with large nesting colonies near the Queen Maud Gulf and on Banks Island. These geese stage during fall in eastern Alberta and western Saskatchewan and concentrate during winter in southeastern Colorado, New Mexico, the Texas Panhandle, and the northern highlands of Mexico (Fig. 19).

WCFP geese wintering in the U.S. portion of their range are surveyed annually, but the entire range, including Mexico, is surveyed only once every 3 years. In the U.S. portion of the survey, 140,600 geese were counted in January 2006, 2% fewer than in 2005 (Fig. 22). These population indices show no trend during 1997-2006 (P = 0.927). During 2006 surveys in Mexico, 87,200 additional WCFP geese were counted, 42% more than in 2003. The total 2006 estimate for WCFP light geese was 227,800, 36% higher than the total estimate in 2003. Indices for the total population indicate an average annual decline of 1% since 1997 (P = 0.808). Species composition surveys indicate that the WCFP was comprised of 63% snow geese and 37% Ross' geese in 2006. Spring break-up was nearly a month earlier than average near Kugluktuk (west of the Queen Maud Gulf), and average spring temperatures throughout western Nunavut reached record highs in 2006. Nesting phenology at the Karrak Lake colony in the Queen Maud Gulf and on Banks Island was about 1 week earlier than average and gosling production there is expected to be above average. Overall, production is expected to be better than average for this population.

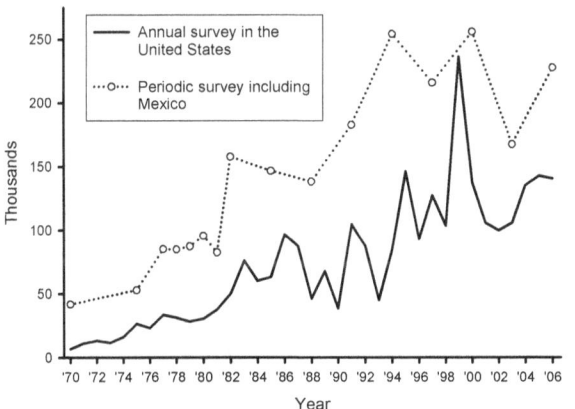

Fig. 22. Estimated number of Western Central Flyway Population light geese counted during winter.

Western Arctic/Wrangel Island Population (WAWI): Most of the snow geese in the Pacific Flyway originate from nesting colonies in the western and central Arctic (WA: Banks Island, the Anderson and Mackenzie River Deltas, and the western Queen Maud Gulf region) or Wrangel Island (WI), located off the northern coast of Russia. The WA segment of the population

winters in central and southern California, New Mexico, and Mexico; the WI segment winters in the Puget Sound area of Washington and in northern and central California (Fig. 19). In winter, WA and WI segments commingle with light geese from other populations in California, complicating surveys.

The fall 2005 estimate of WAWI snow geese was 710,700, 5% lower than the near record high estimated in 2004 (Fig. 23). Fall estimates have increased 7% per year during 1996-2005 (P = 0.003). Nesting phenology on Banks Island was reportedly 1 week earlier than average and production there is expected to be average or better. Surveys indicated that a strong snow goose nesting effort occurred at the Anderson River and Kendall Island colonies. At Wrangel Island's Tundra River colony, nesting phenology was earlier than average in 2006. Preliminary estimates from Wrangel Island include a spring population of 130,000-135,000 adults and 35,000-40,000 nests. Estimates of the Wrangel Island spring population have increased an average of 4% per year since 1997 (P < 0.001). Mean clutch size was 3.7 and the nest predation rate is expected to be low because few foxes were observed in the colony. Biologists expect good production from Wrangel Island in 2006. A cumulative fall flight larger than that of last year is expected.

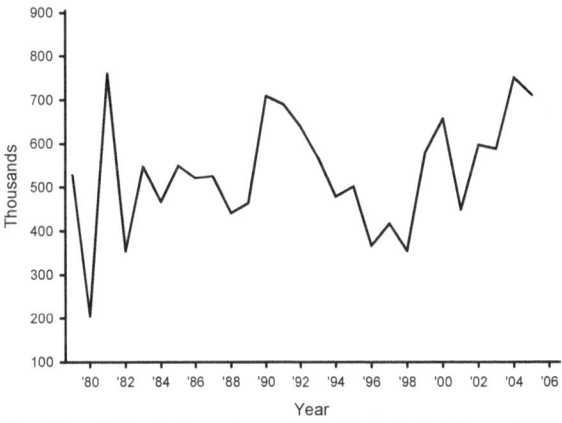

Fig. 23. Estimated number of Western Arctic/Wrangel Island Population light geese during fall.

Greater Snow Geese (GSG): This subspecies principally nests on Bylot, Axel Heiberg, Ellesmere, and Baffin Islands, and on Greenland. These geese winter along the Atlantic coast from New Jersey to North Carolina (Fig. 19).

This population is monitored on their spring staging areas near the St. Lawrence Valley in Quebec. Using the same methodology since 2004, the preliminary estimate from spring 2006 was 1,016,900 (+ 78,700), 25% higher than last year's estimate (P =

0.005, Fig. 24). Spring estimates of greater snow geese have increased an average of 2% per year since 1997 (P = 0.186). The number of snow geese counted during the 2006 MWS in the Atlantic Flyway was 384,700, a 14% increase from the previous survey. Midwinter counts have increased an average of 2% per year during 1997-2006 (P = 0.414). The largest known greater snow goose nesting colony is on Bylot Island. Although snow accumulation was light on the Bylot Island colony this year, cool June weather slightly delayed snowmelt and resulted in lower nesting densities. However, nesting phenology was delayed only 1 day beyond the average. Mean clutch size in 2006 was 4.0, larger than the 3.7 egg average, but the nest predation rate was moderately high. A fall flight similar to that of 2005, but lower than the long-term average is expected.

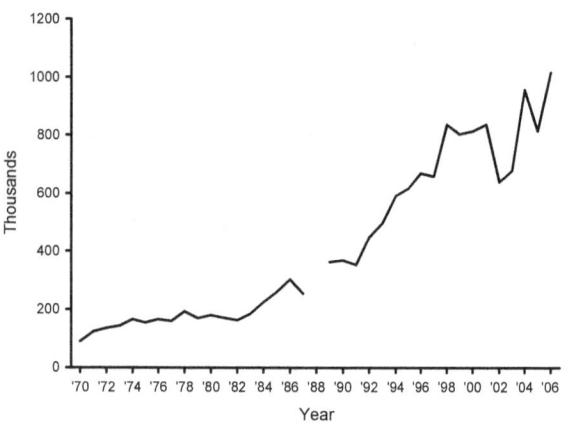

Fig. 24. Estimated number of greater snow geese during spring.

Status of Greater White-fronted Geese

Pacific Population White-fronted Geese (PP): These geese primarily nest on the Yukon-Kuskokwim Delta (YKD) of Alaska and winter in the Central Valley of California (Fig. 19).

The index for this population was a fall estimate from 1979-1998. Since 1999, the index has been a fall population estimate derived from spring surveys of adults on the YKD and Bristol Bay. The 2006 fall estimate is 509,300, 15% higher than the 2005 estimate (Fig. 25). These estimates have increased an average of 3% per year since 1997 (P = 0.041). The spring estimate of total PP white-fronted geese in 2006 was 171,700, an increase of 18% from 2005, and a second consecutive record high (1985-2006). Spring snowmelt on the YKD was about 1 week later than average, but goose nesting phenology was delayed only 2-3 days from the long-term average. The YKD nesting surveys indicated that white-fronted goose nest density, clutch size, and nest success

were above the recent 10-year average. A fall flight similar to last year's large fall flight is expected.

Mid-continent Population White-fronted Geese (MCP): These white-fronted geese nest across a broad region from central and northwestern Alaska to the central Arctic and the Foxe Basin. They concentrate in southern Saskatchewan during the fall and in Texas, Louisiana, Arkansas, and Mexico during winter (Fig. 19).

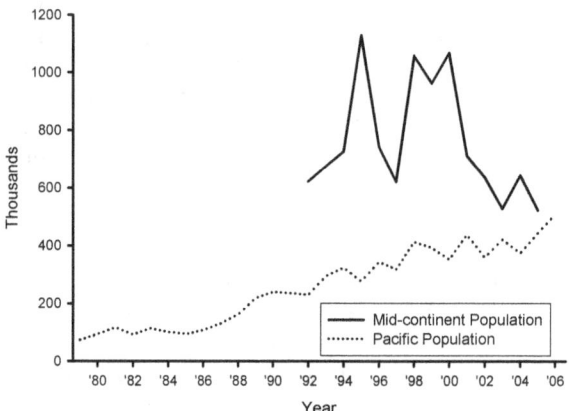

Fig. 25. Estimated number of Mid-continent and Pacific Population greater white-fronted geese during fall.

During the fall 2005 survey in Saskatchewan and Alberta, biologists counted 522,800 MCP geese, a decrease of 19% from the 2004 survey (Fig. 25). During 1996-2005, these estimates have declined an average of 5% per year (P = 0.096). Spring break-up was nearly a month earlier than average near Kugluktuk (west of Queen Maud Gulf), and the average spring temperatures throughout western Nunavut reached record highs in 2006. Goose nesting phenology near Queen Maud Gulf in 2006 was about a week earlier than average and nesting conditions from the Rasmussen Lowlands to Kugluktuk appeared to be favorable. Surveys conducted near the Mackenzie Delta (western Canadian mainland) suggested a modest nesting effort by white-fronted geese there. In Alaska's interior, spring snowmelt varied from near average to 1 week later than average, but substantial flooding was limited to the Koyukuk area. Spring snowmelt on Alaska's North Slope was 5-7 days earlier than average. Production of white-fronted geese throughout most of their range, with the exception of the western Canadian mainland, is expected to be above average. A fall flight lower than that of last year is expected.

Status of Brant

Atlantic Brant (ATLB): Most of this population nests on islands of the eastern Arctic. These brant winter along the Atlantic Coast from Massachusetts to North Carolina (Fig. 19).

The 2006 MWS estimate of brant in the Atlantic Flyway was 146,600, 19% higher than the 2005 estimate (Fig. 26). These estimates have shown no trend for the most recent 10-year period (P = 0.789). Climate records from Baffin, Southampton, and Ellesmere Islands indicate that April, May, and June of 2006 were from 1-4° C warmer than the long-term averages. Biologists on Southampton Island reported that spring snowmelt was about 1 week earlier than recent years. Nesting phenology there appeared to be 3-4 days earlier than in 2005 and 2 weeks earlier than in 2004. Indications of warm spring temperatures and earlier than average spring phenology in 2006 suggest that Atlantic brant production may be above average this year.

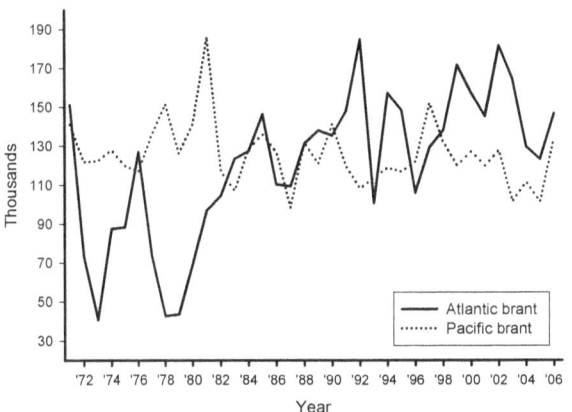

Fig. 26. Estimated number of Atlantic and Pacific Population brant during winter.

Pacific Brant (PACB): These brant nest across Alaska's Yukon-Kuskokwim Delta (YKD) and North Slope, Banks Island, other islands of the western and central Arctic, the Queen Maud Gulf, and Wrangel Island. They winter as far south as Baja California and the west coast of Mexico (Fig. 19).

The 2006 MWS estimate of brant in the Pacific Flyway and Mexico was 133,900, 32% higher than in 2005 (Fig. 26). These estimates have decreased an average of 2% per year during 1997-2006 (P = 0.081). Spring phenology was delayed slightly on the YKD, but was reported as earlier than average on Banks Island and in the Queen Maud Gulf area. Although inland portions of Alaska's North Slope experienced early phenology, coastal areas used by brant were subjected to lingering ice cover. Weather data indicated warmer than average spring

temperatures on Victoria and Ellesmere Islands which should favor nesting efforts. The total brant nesting effort in 2006 decreased in the 5 major YKD colonies (decreased in 3, increased in 2 colonies) compared with previous surveys. Production of brant from the YKD is expected to be reduced from 2005. The fall flight is expected to be somewhat larger than that of last year.

Western High Arctic Brant (WHA): This population of brant nests on the Parry Islands of the Northwest Territories. The population stages in fall at Izembek Lagoon, Alaska. They predominantly winter in Padilla, Samish, and Fidalgo Bays of Washington and near Boundary Bay, British Columbia, although some individuals have been observed as far south as Mexico.

This population is monitored during the MWS in 3 Washington state counties. The 2006 MWS indicated 9,500 brant, 5% fewer than in 2005. These estimates have increased an average of 3% per year during 1997-2006 (P = 0.278). Limited temperature data and satellite imagery suggest that conditions for nesting WHA brant may be improved in 2006 compared to last year.

Status of Emperor Geese

The breeding range of emperor geese is restricted to coastal areas of the Bering Sea, with the largest concentration on the Yukon-Kuskokwim Delta (YKD) in Alaska. Emperor geese migrate relatively short distances and primarily winter in the Aleutian Islands (Fig. 28). Since 1981, emperor geese have been surveyed annually on spring staging areas in southwestern Alaska.

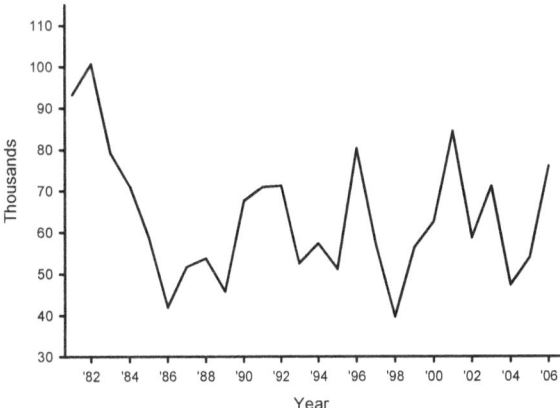

Fig. 27. Estimated numbers of emperor geese present during May surveys.

The spring 2006 emperor goose survey estimate was 76,000 geese, 41% higher than in 2005 (Fig.

27). These estimates have increased an average of 2% per year during 1997-2006 (*P* = 0.350). Spring indices of breeding pairs from the YKD coastal survey declined 6%, but the total bird index increased 15% from 2005 levels. Spring snowmelt on the YKD was about 1 week later than average, but goose nesting phenology was only 2-3 days later than the long-term average. Indices of emperor goose clutch size and nest success on the YKD appeared to be near average. A fall flight similar to that of 2005 is expected.

Status of Tundra Swans

Western Population Tundra Swans: These swans nest along the coastal lowlands of western Alaska, particularly between the Yukon and Kuskokwim Rivers. They winter primarily in California, Utah, and the Pacific Northwest (Fig. 28).

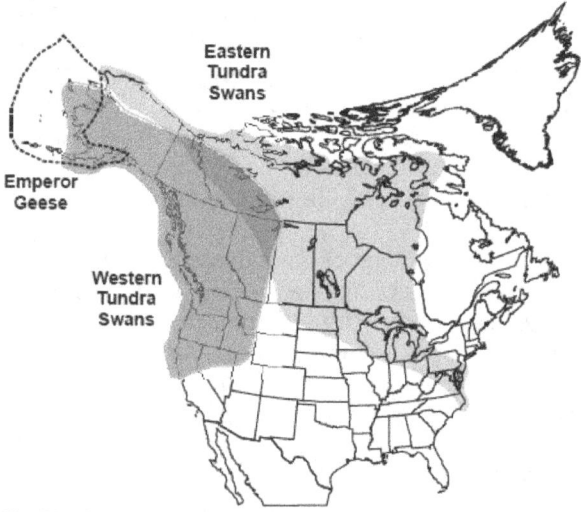

Fig. 28. Approximate range of emperor geese, and eastern and western tundra swan populations in North America.

The 2006 MWS estimate of 106,900 swans was 16% higher than the 2005 estimate (Fig. 29). These estimates have declined by an average of 1% per year during the last 10 years (*P* = 0.796). Spring snowmelt on the YKD was about 1 week later than average, but nesting phenology of most waterfowl there was delayed only 2-3 days from the long-term average. Surveys in the coastal zone of the YKD during spring 2006 indicated substantial increases in total swans (33%), singles and pairs (55%), and swan nests (26%) from respective estimates in 2005. Other western Alaska tundra swan nesting areas experienced spring phenology that was more delayed than the YKD. A fall flight larger than that of last year is expected.

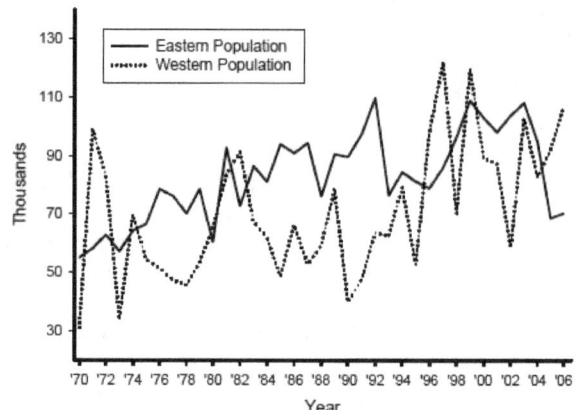

Fig. 29. Estimated numbers of Eastern and Western Population tundra swans during winter.

Eastern Population Tundra Swans: Eastern Population tundra swans nest from the Seward Peninsula of Alaska to the northeast shore of Hudson Bay and Baffin Island. The Mackenzie Delta and adjacent areas are of particular importance. These birds winter in coastal areas from Maryland to North Carolina (Fig. 28).

During the 2006 MWS, 70,500 eastern population tundra swans were observed, 3% more than last year (Fig. 29). These estimates have decreased an average of 3% per year during 1997-2006 (*P* = 0.128). Warmer than average spring temperatures experienced throughout most of Nunavut and Alaska's North Slope should have advanced nesting phenology and benefited Eastern Population tundra swan production in 2006. However, biologists working near the Mackenzie Delta in 2006 encountered only moderate numbers of nesting swans and expected only average production there. Overall, production of eastern population tundra swans in 2006 is expected to be above average.

Appendix A. Individuals who supplied information on the status of ducks.

Alaska, Yukon Territory, and Old Crow Flats (Strata 1-12): B. Conant and E. Mallek

Northern Alberta, Northeastern British Columbia, and Northwest Territories (Strata 13-18, 20, and 77): C. Ferguson and
   D. Benning [d]

Northern Saskatchewan and Northern Manitoba (Strata 21-24): F. Roetker and B. Fortier

Southern and Central Alberta (Strata 26-29, 75, and 76):
   Air   E. Huggins and C. Pyle
   Ground   P. Pryor [a], K. Froggatt [b], S. Barry [a], E. Hofman [b], M. Barr [c], D. Chambers [c], N. Clements [a], N. Fontaine [c],
                J. Going [a], R. Hunka [c], T. Mathews [c], I. McFarlane [c], B. Peers [c], C. Pinto [b], and R. Ta bot [c]

Southern Saskatchewan (Strata 30-35):
   Air   P. Thorpe, T. Lewis, R. King, and S. Frazer
   Ground   D. Nieman [a], J. Smith [a], K. Warner [a], D. Caswell [a], J. Caswell [a], J. Leafloor [a], P. Rakowski [a], M. Schuster [a],
                B. Bartzen [a], K. Dufour [a], C. Downie [a], P. Nieman [a], L. Sitter [a], R. Spencer [a], A. Williams [c], F. Baldwin [a],
                L. Beaudoin [a], S. Lawson [c], C. Meuckon [a], N. Wiebe [a], and K. Wilkins

Southern Manitoba (Strata 25 and 36-40):
   Air   R. King and S. Frazer
   Ground   D. Caswell [a], G. Ball [b], J. Caswell [a], J. Leafloor [a], P. Rakowski [a], M. Schuster [a], F. Baldwin [a], L. Beaudoin [a],
                S. Lawson [c], C. Meuckon [a], N. Wiebe [a], and K. Wilkins

Montana and Western Dakotas (Strata 41-44):
   Air   R. Bentley and K. Richkus
   Ground   P. Garrettson and M. Carpenter

Eastern Dakotas (Strata 45-49):
   Air   J. Solberg and M. Rich
   Ground   K. Kruse, M. Grov jahn [b], B. McDermott, and D. Whittington

Central Quebec (Strata 68-70):
   Air   J. Wortham, D. Fronczak, and G. Boomer
   Helicopter   D. Holtby [b] and G. Boomer

New York, Eastern Ontario, Hudson and James Bay Lowlands of Ontario, and Southern Quebec (Strata 52-59):
   Air   M. Koneff, M. Jones, and R. Raftovich

Central and Western Ontario (Strata 50 and 51):
   Air   K. Bollinger and J. Bredy

Maine and Maritimes (Strata 62-67):
   Air   J. Bidwell, H. Obrecht, and J. Goldsberry [d]

Canadian Wildlife Service helicopter plot survey
   Quebec: D. Bordage [a], C. Lepage [a], S. Orichefsky [a], Y. Côté [d], M. Dubé [d], G. Gagnon [d], and M. Samson [d]
   Ontario: K. Ross [a], D. Fillman [a], and D. McNicol [a]
   New Brunswick and Nova Scotia: B. Pollard [a] and R. Hicks [a]
   Labrador and Newfoundland: S. Gilliland [a], K. Chaulk [a], B. Pollard [a], and W. Barney [a]

British Columbia: A. Breault [b] and participants from the Canadian Wildlife Service, Ducks Unlimited Canada, British Columbia
   Wildlife Branch, Canadian Parks Service, private organizations

California:
   Air   D. Yparraguirre [b] and M. Weaver [b]
   Ground   D. Loughman [d] and J. Laughlin [d]

Michigan: F. McNew [b], B. Barlow [b], S. Chadwick [b], E. Flegler [b], E. Kafcas [b], A. Karr [b], T. Maples [b], J. Niewoonder [b],
                J. Robison [b], B. Scullon [b], B. Sova [b], and V. Weigold [b]

Minnesota:
Air	T. Pfingsten [b] and S. Cordts [b]
Ground	S. Kelly, W. Brininger, J. Holler, J. Kelley, D. Hertel, R. Papasso, T. Rondeau, S. Zodrow, K. Bousquet, B. Boyle, L. Deede, D. Johnson, M, Hanan, R. Martinez, P. Richert, and L. Wolff

Nebraska: M. Vrtiska [b]

Northeastern U.S.:
Data Analysis	R. Raftovich
Connecticut	M. Huang [b] and K. Kub k [b]
Delaware	No survey
Maryland	L. Hindman [b], P. Allen [b] K. Blizzard [b], D. Brinker [b], R. Brown [b], T. Decker [b], K. D'Loughy [b], B. Evans [b], R. Harvey [b], D. Heilmeier [b], R. Hill [b], B. Joyce [b], B. Martin [b], R. Norris [b], D. Price [b], G. Timko [b], and D. Webster [b]
Massachusetts	Massachusetts Division of Fisheries and Wildlife personnel and cooperators.
New Hampshire	Not available.
New Jersey	T. Nichols [b], N. Zimpfer [b], P. Castelli [b], A. Burnett [b], J. Garris [b], B. Kirkpatrick [b], S. Petzinger [b], J. Powers [b], S. Predi [b], L. Widjeskog [b], and D. Wilkinson [b]
New York	New York Department of Environmental Conservation staff.
Pennsylvania	Staff of the Pennsylvania Game Commission and Bureau of Wildlife Management
Rhode Island	J. Osenkowski [b], L. Gibson [b], B. Teft [b], and C, Brown [b]
Vermont	B. Crenshaw [b], T. Appleton [b], J. Austin [b], D. Blodgett [b], J. Buck [b], J. Gobeille [b], F. Hammond [b], J. Mlcuch [b], K. Royar [b], and D. Sausville [b],
Virginia	G. Costanzo [b] and T. Bidrowski [b]

Oregon: B. Bales [b], T. Collom [b], J. Journey [b], M. Kirsch [b], R. Klus [b], D. Marvin [b], E. Miguez [b], R. Prince [b], N. Saake [d], M. St. Louis [b], and Brim Aviation [d]

Wisconsin:
Data	K. Van Horn [b]
Air	L. Waskow [b], P. Beringer [b], C. Cold [b], B. Glenzinski [b], C. Milestone [b], and P. Samerdyke [b]
Ground	T. Aldred [b], T. Bahti [b], K. Benton [b], J. Carstens [b], J. Curry [b], P. David [d], G. Dunsmoor [b], B. Folley [b], G. Gray [b], H. Halverson, B. Hill [b], J. Huff [b], S, Krueger, J. Lutes, D. Matheys [b], R. McDonough [b], R. Mockler, K. Morgan [b], D. North [b], W. Oehmichen [b], S. Otto, S. Papon, J. Robaidek [b], R. Ruwaldt [d], E. Williams [b], M. Windsor [b], G. Van Vreede, and D. Wyman [b]

Habitat information was provided by U.S. Fish and Wildlife Service and Canadian Wildlife Service biologists. Analysis of eastern survey data by John Sauer, U.S. Geological Survey.

[a] Canadian Wildlife Service
[b] State, Provincial, or Tribal Conservation Agency
[c] Ducks Unlimited - Canada
[d] Other organization
All others – U.S. Fish and Wildlife Service

Appendix B. Individuals who supplied information on the status of geese and swans.

Flyway-wide and Regional Survey Reports: D. Caswell[a], B. Conant, K. Dickson[a], J. Fischer, D. Fronczak, K. Gamble, K. Kruse, J. Leafloor[a], R. Oates, M. Otto, R. Raftovich, J. Serie, D. Sharp, and R. Trost

Information from the Breeding Population and Habitat Survey: see Appendix A

North Atlantic Population of Canada Geese: J. Bidwell, and S. Gilliland[a]

Atlantic Population of Canada Geese: J. Bidwell, P. Castelli[b], R. Cotter[a], W. Harvey[b], L. Hindman[b], J. Lefebvre[a], P. May[d], and E. Reed[a]

Atlantic Flyway Resident Population of Canada Geese: P. Castelli[b], G. Costanzo[b], W. Crenshaw[b], J. Dunn[b], H. Heusmann[b], L. Hindman[b], M. Huang[b], K. Jacobs[b], J. Osenkowski[b], R. Raftovich, E. Robinson[b], and T. Whittendale[b]

Southern James Bay Population of Canada Geese: K. Abraham[b], R. Brook[b], J. Hughes[a], M. Koneff, and L. Walton[b]

Mississippi Valley Population of Canada Geese: K. Abraham[b], R. Brook[b], J. Hughes[a], M. Koneff, and L. Walton[b]

Mississippi Flyway Population Giant Canada Geese: K. Abraham[b], D. Graber[b], M. Gillespie[b], R. Helm[b], J. Hopper[b], J. Hughes[a], D. Luukkonen[b], R. Marshalla[b], S. Maxson[b], A. Phelps[b], R. Pritchert[b], M. Shieldcastle[b], K. Van Horn[b], and G. Zenner[b]

Eastern Prairie Population of Canada Geese: D. Andersen[d], M. Gillespie[b], B. Lubinski, A. Raedeke[b], M. Reiter[d], and J. Wollenberg[b]

Western Prairie and Great Plains Populations of Canada Geese: M. Johnson[b], R. King, M. Kraft[b], D. Nieman[a], M. O'Meilia[b], F. Roetker, J. Solberg, P. Thorpe, S. Vaa[b], M. Vritiska[b]

Tall Grass Prairie Population of Canada Geese: R. Alisauskas[a], J. Caswell[d], B. Conant, G. Gilchrist[a], D. Groves, and T. Moser

Short Grass Prairie Population of Canada Geese: R. Alisauskas[a], B. Conant, C. Ferguson, D. Graber[b], D. Groves, J. Hines[a], T. Moser, and J. Rausch[a]

Hi-Line Population of Canada Geese: R. Bentley, J. Dubovsky, J. Gammonley[b], J. Hansen[b], E. Huggins, D. Nieman[a], L. Roberts[b], and P. Thorpe

Rocky Mountain Population of Canada Geese: T. Aldrich[b], R. Bentley, J. Bohne[b], J. Dubovsky, E. Huggins, C. Mortimore[b], R. Northrup[b], L. Roberts[b], T. Sanders[b], and D. Yparraguirre[b]

Pacific Population of Canada Geese: A. Breault[a], B. Bales[b], C. Ferguson, T. Hemker[b], E. Huggins, R. Northrup[b], D. Kraege[b], C. Mortimore[b], M. Weaver[b], and D. Yparraguirre[b]

Dusky Canada Geese: B. Eldridge, B. Larned, D. Logan[d], and T. Rothe[b]

Lesser and Taverner's Canada Geese: B. Conant, C. Dau, B. Larned, and E. Mallek

Cackling Canada Geese: M. Anthony[d], C. Dau, B. Eldridge, and M. Wege

Aleutian Canada Geese: V. Byrd

Greater Snow Geese: J. Lefebvre[a], G. Gauthier[d], and A. Reed[a]

Mid-continent Population Light Geese: K. Abraham[b], J. Caswell[d], G. Gilchrist[a], B. Lubinski, A. Raedeke[b], R. Rockwell[d], L. Walton[b], and J. Wollenberg[b]

Western Central Flyway Population Light Geese: R. Alisauskas[a], J. Hines[a], K. Kruse, T. Moser, J. Rausch[a], and P. Thorpe

Western Arctic/Wrangel Island Population of Lesser Snow Geese: V. Baranuk[d], S. Boyd[a], J. Hines[a], and D. Kraege[b]

Ross' Geese: R. Alisauskas[a], J. Caswell[d], J. Leafloor[a], and P. Thorpe

Pacific Population White-Fronted Geese: C. Dau, B. Eldridge, and D. Groves

Mid-continent Population White-fronted Geese: R. Alisauskas[a], B. Conant, S. Durham[b], D. Groves, J. Hines[a], S. Kovach, B. Larned, D. Lobpries[b], N. Lyman[b], E. Mallek, D. Nieman[a], F. Roetker, J. Smith[a], J. Solberg, M. Spindler, R. Walters[b], and K. Warner[a]

Pacific Brant: M. Anthony[d], B. Eldridge, and R. King

Atlantic Brant: I. Butler[d], G. Gilchrist[a], M. Kay[a], and R. Ludkin[d]

Western High Arctic Brant: D. Kraege[b]

Emperor Geese: C. Dau, B. Eldridge, R. King, and E. Mallek

Western Population of Tundra Swans: C. Dau, and B. Eldridge

Eastern Population of Tundra Swans: C. Dau, J. Hines[a], B. Larned, and E. Mallek

---

[a]Canadian Wildlife Service.
[b]State, Provincial, or Tribal Conservation Agency.
[c]Ducks Unlimited – Canada.
[d]Other organization.
All others - U.S. Fish and Wildlife Service.

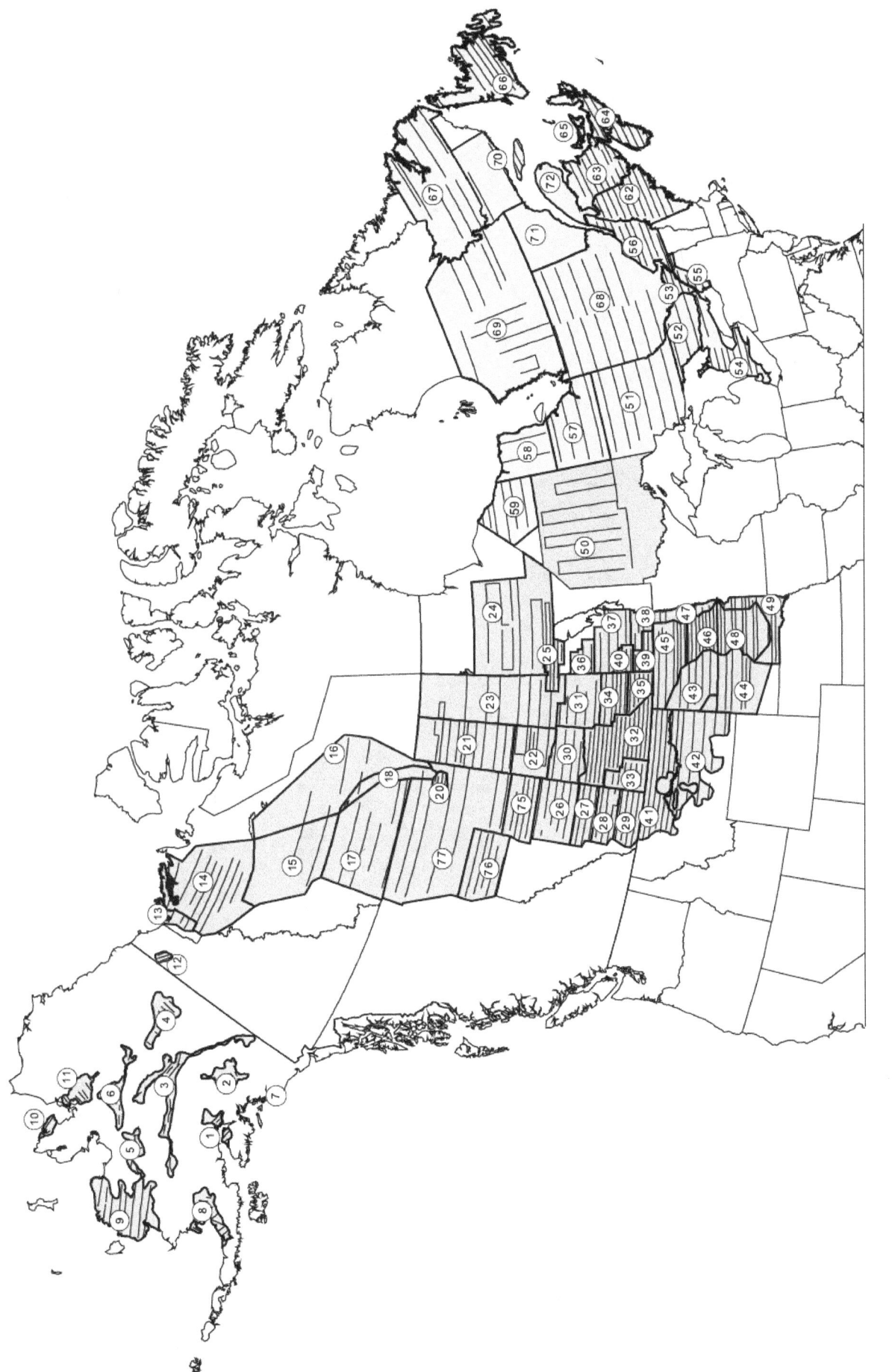

Appendix C. Strata and transects of the Waterfowl Breeding Population and Habitat Survey (gray = traditional survey area, blue = eastern survey area).

Appendix D. Estimated number of May ponds and standard errors (in thousands) in portions of Prairie Canada and the northcentral U.S.

Year	Prairie Canada $\hat{N}$	Prairie Canada $\hat{SE}$	Northcentral U.S.[a] $\hat{N}$	Northcentral U.S.[a] $\hat{SE}$	Total $\hat{N}$	Total $\hat{SE}$
1961	1977.2	165.4				
1962	2369.1	184.6				
1963	2482.0	129.3				
1964	3370.7	173.0				
1965	4378.8	212.2				
1966	4554.5	229.3				
1967	4691.2	272.1				
1968	1985.7	120.2				
1969	3547.6	221.9				
1970	4875.0	251.2				
1971	4053.4	200.4				
1972	4009.2	250.9				
1973	2949.5	197.6				
1974	6390.1	308.3	1840.8	197.2	8230.9	366.0
1975	5320.1	271.3	1910.8	116.1	7230.9	295.1
1976	4598.8	197.1	1391.5	99.2	5990.3	220.7
1977	2277.9	120.7	771.1	51.1	3049.1	131.1
1978	3622.1	158.0	1590.4	81.7	5212.4	177.9
1979	4858.9	252.0	1522.2	70.9	6381.1	261.8
1980	2140.9	107.7	761.4	35.8	2902.3	113.5
1981	1443.0	75.3	682.8	34.0	2125.8	82.6
1982	3184.9	178.6	1458.0	86.4	4642.8	198.4
1983	3905.7	208.2	1259.2	68.7	5164.9	219.2
1984	2473.1	196.6	1766.2	90.8	4239.3	216.5
1985	4283.1	244.1	1326.9	74.0	5610.0	255.1
1986	4024.7	174.4	1734.8	74.4	5759.5	189.6
1987	2523.7	131.0	1347.8	46.8	3871.5	139.1
1988	2110.1	132.4	790.7	39.4	2900.8	138.1
1989	1692.7	89.1	1289.9	61.7	2982.7	108.4
1990	2817.3	138.3	691.2	45.9	3508.5	145.7
1991	2493.9	110.2	706.1	33.6	3200.0	115.2
1992	2783.9	141.6	825.0	30.8	3608.9	144.9
1993	2261.1	94.0	1350.6	57.1	3611.7	110.0
1994	3769.1	173.9	2215.6	88.8	5984.8	195.3
1995	3892.5	223.8	2442.9	106.8	6335.4	248.0
1996	5002.6	184.9	2479.7	135.3	7482.2	229.1
1997	5061.0	180.3	2397.2	94.4	7458.2	203.5
1998	2521.7	133.8	2065.3	89.2	4586.9	160.8
1999	3862.0	157.2	2842.3	256.8	6704.3	301.1
2000	2422.2	96.1	1524.5	99.9	3946.9	138.6
2001	2747.2	115.6	1893.2	91.5	4640.4	147.4
2002	1439.0	105.0	1281.1	63.4	2720.0	122.7
2003	3522.3	151.8	1667.8	67.4	5190.1	166.1
2004	2512.6	131.0	1407.0	101.7	3919.6	165.8
2005	3920.5	196.7	1460.7	79.7	5381.2	212.2
2006	4449.5	221.5	1644.4	85.4	6093.9	237.4

[a] No comparable survey data available for the northcentral U.S. during 1961-73.

Appendix E. Breeding population estimates (in thousands) for total ducks[a] and mallards for states, provinces, or regions that conduct spring surveys.

Year	British Columbia[b] Total ducks	Mallards	California Total ducks	Mallards	Michigan Total ducks	Mallards	Minnesota Total ducks	Mallards	Nebraska Total ducks	Mallards
1955									101.5	32.0
1956									94.9	25.8
1957									154.8	26.8
1958									176.4	28.1
1959									99.7	12.1
1960									143.6	21.6
1961									141.8	43.3
1962									68.9	35.8
1963									114.9	37.4
1964									124.8	66.8
1965									52.9	20.8
1966									118.8	36.0
1967									96.2	27.6
1968							368.5	83.7	96.5	24.1
1969							345.3	88.8	100.6	26.7
1970							343.8	113.9	112.4	24.5
1971							286.9	78.5	96.0	22.3
1972							237.6	62.2	91.7	15.2
1973							415.6	99.8	85.5	19.0
1974							332.8	72.8	67.4	19.5
1975							503.3	175.8	62.6	14.8
1976							759.4	117.8	87.2	20.1
1977							536.6	134.2	152.4	24.1
1978							511.3	146.8	126.0	29.0
1979							901.4	158.7	143.8	33.6
1980							740.7	172.0	133.4	37.3
1981							515.2	154.8	66.2	19.4
1982							558.4	120.5	73.2	22.3
1983							394.2	155.8	141.6	32.2
1984							563.8	188.1	154.1	36.1
1985							580.3	216.9	75.4	28.4
1986							537.5	233.6	69.5	15.1
1987	2.7	0.2					614.9	192.3	120.5	41.7
1988	4.9	0.6					752.8	271.7	126.5	27.8
1989	4.6	0.5					1021.6	273.0	136.7	18.7
1990	4.7	0.5					886.8	232.1	81.4	14.7
1991	5.9	0.6					868.2	225.0	126.3	26.0
1992	6.2	0.6	497.4	375.8	665.8	384.0	1127.3	360.9	63.4	24.4
1993	5.7	0.5	666.7	359.0	813.5	454.3	875.9	305.8	92.8	23.8
1994	6.6	0.6	483.2	311.7	848.3	440.6	1320.1	426.5	118.9	17.5
1995	6.5	0.8	589.7	368.5	812.6	559.8	912.2	319.4	142.9	42.0
1996	6.4	0.5	843.7	536.7	790.2	395.8	1062.4	314.8	132.3	38.9
1997	5.7	0.5	824.3	511.3	886.3	489.3	953.0	407.4	128.3	26.1
1998	7.3	0.9	706.8	353.9	1305.2	567.1	739.6	368.5	155.7	43.4
1999	8.5	0.9	851.0	560.1	824.8	494.3	716.5	316.4	251.2[c]	81.1
2000	8.2	0.8	562.4	347.6	1121.7	462.8	815.3	318.1	178.8	54.3
2001	7.8	0.8	413.5	302.2	673.5	358.2	761.3	320.6	225.3	69.2
2002	9.0	0.6	392.0	265.3	997.3	336.8	1224.1	366.6	141.8	50.6
2003	8.6	0.6	533.7	337.1	587.2	294.1	748.9	280.5	96.7	32.9
2004	6.6	0.6	412.8	262.4	701.9	328.8	1099.3	375.3	69.9	23.2
2005	5.6	0.5	615.2	317.9	442.6	238.5	681.3	238.5	117.1	29.3
2006	7.8	0.4	649.4	399.4	353.5	207.8	529.4	160.7		

[a] Species composition for the total duck estimate varies by region.
[b] Index to waterfowl use in prime waterfowl producing areas of the province.
[c] Blanks denote that the survey was not conducted, results were not available, or survey methods changed.
[c] First year of survey after major changes in survey me hodology. Hence, results from earlier years are not comparable.

Year	Nevada Total ducks	Nevada Mallards	Northeastern U.S.[d] Total ducks	Northeastern U.S.[d] Mallards	Oregon Total ducks	Oregon Mallards	Washington Total ducks	Washington Mallards	Wisconsin Total ducks	Wisconsin Mallards
1955										
1956										
1957										
1958										
1959	14.2	2.1								
1960	14.1	2.1								
1961	13.5	2.0								
1962	13.8	1.7								
1963	23.8	2.2								
1964	23.5	3.0								
1965	29.3	3.5								
1966	25.7	3.4								
1967	11.4	1.5								
1968	10.5	1.2								
1969	18.2	1.4								
1970	19.6	1.5								
1971	18.3	1.1								
1972	19.0	0.9								
1973	20.7	0.7								412.7[f]	107.0
1974	17.1	0.7							435.2	94.3
1975	14.5	0.6							426.9	120.5
1976	13.6	0.6							379.5	109.9
1977	16.5	1.0							323.3	91.7
1978	11.1	0.6							271.3	61.6
1979	12.8	0.6					98.6	32.1	265.7	78.6
1980	16.6	0.9					113.7	34.1	248.1	116.5
1981	26.9	1.6					148.3	41.8	505.0	142.8
1982	21.0	1.1					146.4	49.8	218.7	89.5
1983	24.3	1.5					149.5	47.6	202.3	119.5
1984	24.0	1.4					196.3	59.3	210.0	104.8
1985	24.9	1.5					216.2	63.1	192.8	73.9
1986	26.4	1.3					203.8	60.8	262.0	110.8
1987	33.4	1.5					183.6	58.3	389.8	136.9
1988	31.7	1.3					241.8	67.2	287.1	148.9
1989	18.8	1.3					162.3	49.8	462.5	180.7
1990	22.2	1.3					168.9	56.9	328.6	151.4
1991	14.6	1.4					140.8	43.7	435.8	172.4
1992	12.4	0.9					116.3	41.0	683.8	249.7
1993	14.1	1.2	1158.1	686.6			149.8	55.0	379.4	174.5
1994	19.2	1.4	1297.3	856.3	335.6	124.1	123.9	52.7	571.2	283.4
1995	17.9	1.0	1408.5	864.1	227.3	85.3	147.3	58.9	592.4	242.2
1996	26.4	1.7	1430.9	848.6	298.0	107.8	163.3	61.6	536.3	314.4
1997	25.3	2.5	1423.5	795.2	370.3	127.3	172.8	67.0	409.3	181.0
1998	27.9	2.1	1444.0	775.2	357.0	132.3	185.3	79.0	412.8	186.9
1999	29.9	2.3	1522.7	880.0	333.4	133.1	200.2	86.2	476.6	248.4
2000	26.1	2.1	1933.5	762.6	324.0	115.9	143.6	47.7	744.4	454.0
2001	22.2	2.0	1397.4	809.4			146.4	50.5	440.1	183.5
2002	11.7	0.7	1466.2	833.7	275.3	111.7	133.3	44.7	740.8	378.5
2003	21.1	1.7	1266.2	731.9	258.7	96.9	127.8	39.8	533.5	261.3
2004	12.0	1.7	1416.9	805.9	245.0	91.9	114.9	40.0	651.5	229.2
2005	10.7	0.7	1416.2	753.6	225.3	83.0	111.5	40.8	724.3	317.2
2006			1392.1	725.2	263.5	87.9			522.6	219.5

[d] Includes all or portions of Connecticut, Delaware, Maryland, Massachusetts, New Hampshire, New Jersey, New York, Pennsylvania, Rhode Island, Vermont, and Virginia.

Appendix F. Breeding population estimates and standard errors (in thousands) for 10 species of ducks from the traditional survey area (strata 1-18, 20-50, 75-77).

	Mallard		Gadwall		American wigeon		Green-winged teal		Blue-winged teal	
Year	$\hat{N}$	$\hat{SE}$	$\hat{N}$	$\hat{SE}$	$\hat{N}$	$\hat{SE}$	$\hat{N}$	$\hat{SE}$	$\hat{N}$	$\hat{SE}$
1955	8777.3	457.1	651.5	149.5	3216.8	297.8	1807.2	291.5	5305.2	567.6
1956	10452.7	461.8	772.6	142.4	3145.0	227.8	1525.3	236.2	4997.6	527.6
1957	9296.9	443.5	666.8	148.2	2919.8	291.5	1102.9	161.2	4299.5	467.3
1958	11234.2	555.6	502.0	89.6	2551.7	177.9	1347.4	212.2	5456.6	483.7
1959	9024.3	466.6	590.0	72.7	3787.7	339.2	2653.4	459.3	5099.3	332.7
1960	7371.7	354.1	784.1	68.4	2987.6	407.0	1426.9	311.0	4293.0	294.3
1961	7330.0	510.5	654.8	77.5	3048.3	319.9	1729.3	251.5	3655.3	298.7
1962	5535.9	426.9	905.1	87.0	1958.7	145.4	722.9	117.6	3011.1	209.8
1963	6748.8	326.8	1055.3	89.5	1830.8	169.9	1242.3	226.9	3723.6	323.0
1964	6063.9	385.3	873.4	73.7	2589.6	259.7	1561.3	244.7	4020.6	320.4
1965	5131.7	274.8	1260.3	114.8	2301.1	189.4	1282.0	151.0	3594.5	270.4
1966	6731.9	311.4	1680.4	132.4	2318.4	139.2	1617.3	173.6	3733.2	233.6
1967	7509.5	338.2	1384.6	97.8	2325.5	136.2	1593.7	165.7	4491.5	305.7
1968	7089.2	340.8	1949.0	213.9	2298.6	156.1	1430.9	146.6	3462.5	389.1
1969	7531.6	280.2	1573.4	100.2	2941.4	168.6	1491.0	103.5	4138.6	239.5
1970	9985.9	617.2	1608.1	123.5	3469.9	318.5	2182.5	137.7	4861.8	372.3
1971	9416.4	459.5	1605.6	123.0	3272.9	186.2	1889.3	132.9	4610.2	322.8
1972	9265.5	363.9	1622.9	120.1	3200.1	194.1	1948.2	185.8	4278.5	230.5
1973	8079.2	377.5	1245.6	90.3	2877.9	197.4	1949.2	131.9	3332.5	220.3
1974	6880.2	351.8	1592.4	128.2	2672.0	159.3	1864.5	131.2	4976.2	394.6
1975	7726.9	344.1	1643.9	109.0	2778.3	192.0	1664.8	148.1	5885.4	337.4
1976	7933.6	337.4	1244.8	85.7	2505.2	152.7	1547.5	134.0	4744.7	294.5
1977	7397.1	381.8	1299.0	126.4	2575.1	185.9	1285.8	87.9	4462.8	328.4
1978	7425.0	307.0	1558.0	92.2	3282.4	208.0	2174.2	219.1	4498.6	293.3
1979	7883.4	327.0	1757.9	121.0	3106.5	198.2	2071.7	198.5	4875.9	297.6
1980	7706.5	307.2	1392.9	98.8	3595.5	213.2	2049.9	140.7	4895.1	295.6
1981	6409.7	308.4	1395.4	120.0	2946.0	173.0	1910.5	141.7	3720.6	242.1
1982	6408.5	302.2	1633.8	126.2	2458.7	167.3	1535.7	140.2	3657.6	203.7
1983	6456.0	286.9	1519.2	144.3	2636.2	181.4	1875.0	148.0	3366.5	197.2
1984	5415.3	258.4	1515.0	125.0	3002.2	174.2	1408.2	91.5	3979.3	267.6
1985	4960.9	234.7	1303.0	98.2	2050.7	143.7	1475.4	100.3	3502.4	246.3
1986	6124.2	241.6	1547.1	107.5	1736.5	109.9	1674.9	136.1	4478.8	237.1
1987	5789.8	217.9	1305.6	97.1	2012.5	134.3	2006.2	180.4	3528.7	220.2
1988	6369.3	310.3	1349.9	121.1	2211.1	139.1	2060.8	188.3	4011.1	290.4
1989	5645.4	244.1	1414.6	106.6	1972.9	106.0	1841.7	166.4	3125.3	229.8
1990	5452.4	238.6	1672.1	135.8	1860.1	108.3	1789.5	172.7	2776.4	178.7
1991	5444.6	205.6	1583.7	111.8	2254.0	139.5	1557.8	111.3	3763.7	270.8
1992	5976.1	241.0	2032.8	143.4	2208.4	131.9	1773.1	123.7	4333.1	263.2
1993	5708.3	208.9	1755.2	107.9	2053.0	109.3	1694.5	112.7	3192.9	205.6
1994	6980.1	282.8	2318.3	145.2	2382.2	130.3	2108.4	152.2	4616.2	259.2
1995	8269.4	287.5	2835.7	187.5	2614.5	136.3	2300.6	140.3	5140.0	253.3
1996	7941.3	262.9	2984.0	152.5	2271.7	125.4	2499.5	153.4	6407.4	353.9
1997	9939.7	308.5	3897.2	264.9	3117.6	161.6	2506.6	142.5	6124.3	330.7
1998	9640.4	301.6	3742.2	205.6	2857.7	145.3	2087.3	138.9	6398.8	332.3
1999	10805.7	344.5	3235.5	163.8	2920.1	185.5	2631.0	174.6	7149.5	364.5
2000	9470.2	290.2	3158.4	200.7	2733.1	138.8	3193.5	200.1	7431.4	425.0
2001	7904.0	226.9	2679.2	136.1	2493.5	149.6	2508.7	156.4	5757.0	288.8
2002	7503.7	246.5	2235.4	135.4	2334.4	137.9	2333.5	143.8	4206.5	227.9
2003	7949.7	267.3	2549.0	169.9	2551.4	156.9	2678.5	199.7	5518.2	312.7
2004	7425.3	282.0	2589.6	165.6	1981.3	114.9	2460.8	145.2	4073.0	238.0
2005	6755.3	280.8	2179.1	131.0	2225.1	139.2	2156.9	125.8	4585.5	236.3
2006	7276.5	223.7	2824.7	174.2	2171.2	115.7	2587.2	155.3	5859.6	303.5

Year	Northern shoveler $\hat{N}$	$\hat{SE}$	Northern pintail $\hat{N}$	$\hat{SE}$	Redhead $\hat{N}$	$\hat{SE}$	Canvasback $\hat{N}$	$\hat{SE}$	Scaup $\hat{N}$	$\hat{SE}$
1955	1642.8	218.7	9775.1	656.1	539.9	98.9	589.3	87.8	5620.1	582.1
1956	1781.4	196.4	10372.8	694.4	757.3	119.3	698.5	93.3	5994.1	434.0
1957	1476.1	181.8	6606.9	493.4	509.1	95.7	626.1	94.7	5766.9	411.7
1958	1383.8	185.1	6037.9	447.9	457.1	66.2	746.8	96.1	5350.4	355.1
1959	1577.6	301.1	5872.7	371.6	498.8	55.5	488.7	50.6	7037.6	492.3
1960	1824.5	130.1	5722.2	323.2	497.8	67.0	605.7	82.4	4868.6	362.5
1961	1383.0	166.5	4218.2	496.2	323.3	38.8	435.3	65.7	5380.0	442.2
1962	1269.0	113.9	3623.5	243.1	507.5	60.0	360.2	43.8	5286.1	426.4
1963	1398.4	143.8	3846.0	255.6	413.4	61.9	506.2	74.9	5438.4	357.9
1964	1718.3	240.3	3291.2	239.4	528.1	67.3	643.6	126.9	5131.8	386.1
1965	1423.7	114.1	3591.9	221.9	599.3	77.7	522.1	52.8	4640.0	411.2
1966	2147.0	163.9	4811.9	265.6	713.1	77.6	663.1	78.0	4439.2	356.2
1967	2314.7	154.6	5277.7	341.9	735.7	79.0	502.6	45.4	4927.7	456.1
1968	1684.5	176.8	3489.4	244.6	499.4	53.6	563.7	101.3	4412.7	351.8
1969	2156.8	117.2	5903.9	296.2	633.2	53.6	503.5	53.7	5139.8	378.5
1970	2230.4	117.4	6392.0	396.7	622.3	64.3	580.1	90.4	5662.5	391.4
1971	2011.4	122.7	5847.2	368.1	534.4	57.0	450.7	55.2	5143.3	333.8
1972	2466.5	182.8	6979.0	364.5	550.9	49.4	425.9	46.0	7997.0	718.0
1973	1619.0	112.2	4356.2	267.0	500.8	57.7	620.5	89.1	6257.4	523.1
1974	2011.3	129.9	6598.2	345.8	626.3	70.8	512.8	56.8	5780.5	409.8
1975	1980.8	106.7	5900.4	267.3	831.9	93.5	595.1	56.1	6460.0	486.0
1976	1748.1	106.9	5475.6	299.2	665.9	66.3	614.4	70.1	5818.7	348.7
1977	1451.8	82.1	3926.1	246.8	634.0	79.9	664.0	74.9	6260.2	362.8
1978	1975.3	115.6	5108.2	267.8	724.6	62.2	373.2	41.5	5984.4	403.0
1979	2406.5	135.6	5376.1	274.4	697.5	63.8	582.0	59.8	7657.9	548.6
1980	1908.2	119.9	4508.1	228.6	728.4	116.7	734.6	83.8	6381.7	421.2
1981	2333.6	177.4	3479.5	260.5	594.9	62.0	620.8	59.1	5990.9	414.2
1982	2147.6	121.7	3708.8	226.6	616.9	74.2	513.3	50.9	5532.0	380.9
1983	1875.7	105.3	3510.6	178.1	711.9	83.3	526.6	58.9	7173.8	494.9
1984	1618.2	91.9	2964.8	166.8	671.3	72.0	530.1	60.1	7024.3	484.7
1985	1702.1	125.7	2515.5	143.0	578.2	67.1	375.9	42.9	5098.0	333.1
1986	2128.2	112.0	2739.7	152.1	559.6	60.5	438.3	41.5	5235.3	355.5
1987	1950.2	118.4	2628.3	159.4	502.4	54.9	450.1	77.9	4862.7	303.8
1988	1680.9	210.4	2005.5	164.0	441.9	66.2	435.0	40.2	4671.4	309.5
1989	1538.3	95.9	2111.9	181.3	510.7	58.5	477.4	48.4	4342.1	291.3
1990	1759.3	118.6	2256.6	183.3	480.9	48.2	539.3	60.3	4293.1	264.9
1991	1716.2	104.6	1803.4	131.3	445.6	42.1	491.2	66.4	5254.9	364.9
1992	1954.4	132.1	2098.1	161.0	595.6	69.7	481.5	97.3	4639.2	291.9
1993	2046.5	114.3	2053.4	124.2	485.4	53.1	472.1	67.6	4080.1	249.4
1994	2912.0	141.4	2972.3	188.0	653.5	66.7	525.6	71.1	4529.0	253.6
1995	2854.9	150.3	2757.9	177.6	888.5	90.6	770.6	92.2	4446.4	277.6
1996	3449.0	165.7	2735.9	147.5	834.2	83.1	848.5	118.3	4217.4	234.5
1997	4120.4	194.0	3558.0	194.2	918.3	77.2	688.8	57.2	4112.3	224.2
1998	3183.2	156.5	2520.6	136.8	1005.1	122.9	685.9	63.8	3471.9	191.2
1999	3889.5	202.1	3057.9	230.5	973.4	69.5	716.0	79.1	4411.7	227.9
2000	3520.7	197.9	2907.6	170.5	926.3	78.1	706.8	81.0	4026.3	205.3
2001	3313.5	166.8	3296.0	266.6	712.0	70.2	579.8	52.7	3694.0	214.9
2002	2318.2	125.6	1789.7	125.2	564.8	69.0	486.6	43.8	3524.1	210.3
2003	3619.6	221.4	2558.2	174.8	636.8	56.6	557.6	48.0	3734.4	225.5
2004	2810.4	163.9	2184.6	155.2	605.3	51.5	617.2	64.6	3807.2	202.3
2005	3591.5	178.6	2560.5	146.8	592.3	51.7	520.6	52.9	3386.9	196.4
2006	3680.2	236.5	3386.4	198.7	916.3	86.1	691.0	69.6	3246.7	166.9

Appendix G. Total breeding duck estimates for the traditional survey area, in thousands.

| Year | Traditional survey area [a] | |
	$\hat{N}$	$\hat{SE}$
1955	39603.6	1264.0
1956	42035.2	1177.3
1957	34197.1	1016.6
1958	36528.1	1013.6
1959	40089.9	1103.6
1960	32080.5	876.8
1961	29829.0	1009.0
1962	25038.9	740.6
1963	27609.5	736.6
1964	27768.8	827.5
1965	25903.1	694.4
1966	30574.2	689.5
1967	32688.6	796.1
1968	28971.2	789.4
1969	33760.9	674.6
1970	39676.3	1008.1
1971	36905.1	821.8
1972	40748.0	987.1
1973	32573.9	805.3
1974	35422.5	819.5
1975	37792.8	836.2
1976	34342.3	707.8
1977	32049.0	743.8
1978	35505.6	745.4
1979	38622.0	843.4
1980	36224.4	737.9
1981	32267.3	734.9
1982	30784.0	678.8
1983	32635.2	725.8
1984	31004.9	716.5
1985	25638.3	574.9
1986	29092.8	609.3
1987	27412.1	562.1
1988	27361.7	660.8
1989	25112.8	555.4
1990	25079.2	539.9
1991	26605.6	588.7
1992	29417.9	605.6
1993	26312.4	493.9
1994	32523.5	598.2
1995	35869.6	629.4
1996	37753.0	779.6
1997	42556.3	718.9
1998	39081.9	652.0
1999	43435.8	733.9
2000	41838.3	740.2
2001	36177.5	633.1
2002	31181.1	547.8
2003	36225.1	664.7
2006	36160.3	614.4

[a] Total ducks in the traditional survey area include species in Appx. F plus black duck, ring-necked duck, goldeneyes, bufflehead, and ruddy duck.

Appendix H. Breeding population estimates and 95% confidence intervals or credibility intervals (CIs; in thousands) for the 10 most abundant species of ducks in the eastern survey area [a].

	Mergansers [b]		Mallard		American black duck		American wigeon		Green-winged teal	
Year	$\hat{N}$	95% CI	$\hat{N}$	95% CI	$\hat{N}$	95% CI	$\hat{N}$	95% CI	$\hat{N}$	95% CI
1990	301.7	(247.4, 356.0)	312.8	(186.3, 570.8)	426.9	(370.4, 498.1)	12.2	(0.0, 26.3)	219.2	(163.3, 305.1)
1991	393.9	(320.8, 467.0)	352.0	(211.4, 628.8)	419.1	(359.2, 495.6)	9.8	(2.5, 17.1)	209.5	(156.1, 293.9)
1992	332.4	(259.3, 405.5)	355.5	(209.8, 648.2)	402.5	(348.1, 471.4)	4.7	(0.0, 9.4)	198.6	(147.0, 275.2)
1993	274.7	(213.2, 336.2)	353.1	(210.3, 638.5)	402.5	(344.3, 473.6)	10.8	(1.4, 20.2)	178.5	(130.7, 251.9)
1994	327.5	(256.4, 398.6)	374.1	(221.4, 680.3)	369.3	(314.3, 434.9)	10.0	(0.0, 20.4)	190.0	(139.4, 269.5)
1995	293.0	(236.2, 349.8)	311.4	(183.4, 581.8)	416.7	(354.6, 491.6)	8.6	(0.0, 22.5)	194.9	(142.8, 278.9)
1996	318.8	(263.3, 374.3)	329.7	(195.3, 604.5)	488.7	(427.9, 564.6)	9.4	(2.1, 16.7)	257.3	(194.5, 355.5)
1997	392.9	(322.7, 463.1)	347.1	(202.4, 635.1)	451.1	(395.6, 517.9)	15.0	(6.4, 23.6)	200.6	(152.0, 275.5)
1998	308.7	(237.0, 380.4)	384.0	(230.2, 682.9)	482.7	(425.7, 554.9)	14.9	(1.6, 28.2)	197.2	(149.7, 267.9)
1999	378.9	(258.6, 499.2)	394.3	(237.1, 700.3)	526.8	(462.4, 605.8)	5.2	(1.7, 8.7)	228.2	(169.8, 315.2)
2000	375.3	(313.0, 437.6)	344.2	(207.4, 622.9)	504.2	(442.9, 576.2)	14.5	(2.7, 26.3)	248.5	(190.1, 336.4)
2001	373.8	(306.8, 440.8)	380.8	(232.3, 684.6)	472.7	(415.3, 540.3)	8.9	(3.6, 14.2)	208.5	(158.4, 284.0)
2002	557.4	(444.1, 670.7)	371.1	(226.7, 666.1)	522.6	(459.3, 599.9)	8.9	(2.6, 15.2)	249.6	(188.2, 345.0)
2003	460.1	(340.7, 579.5)	393.4	(236.8, 713.7)	474.4	(416.4, 544.0)	11.5	(0.0, 24.2)	234.5	(177.0, 324.8)
2004	455.2	(378.6, 531.8)	418.6	(255.1, 737.4)	487.8	(429.4, 558.3)	15.4	(1.1, 29.7)	273.2	(204.2, 379.4)
2005	418.4	(334.9, 501.9)	401.8	(239.8, 721.9)	472.0	(413.9, 544.2)	16.2	(8.4, 24.0)	223.3	(168.9, 306.3)
2006	448.2	(344.3, 552.1)	371.0	(225.6, 661.9)	490.3	(430.4, 563.2)	7.9	(2.2, 13.6)	223.0	(168.8, 305.6)

	Scaup [c]		Ring-necked duck		Goldeneyes [d]		Bufflehead		Scoters [e]	
Year	$\hat{N}$	95% CI	$\hat{N}$	95% CI	$\hat{N}$	95% CI	$\hat{N}$	95% CI	$\hat{N}$	95% CI
1990	48.4	(0.0, 104.1)	513.7	(392.4, 695.7)	309.8	(134.0, 485.6)	38.1	(24.6, 51.6)	97.4	(0.0, 216.8)
1991	33.8	(8.3, 59.3)	457.7	(352.2, 615.3)	303.7	(152.0, 455.4)	29.2	(13.1, 45.3)	89.8	(15.5, 164.1)
1992	36.7	(0.0, 76.1)	454.2	(350.9, 604.2)	306.1	(166.7, 445.5)	27.7	(16.9, 38.5)	80.4	(0.0, 206.4)
1993	7.1	(1.0, 13.2)	417.4	(321.5, 555.9)	306.2	(119.6, 492.8)	6.4	(2.3, 10 5)	104.4	(1.3, 207 5)
1994	36.4	(0.3, 72.5)	431.8	(329.9, 579.7)	227.2	(119.6, 334.8)	12.1	(0.0, 26.4)	73.5	(4.7, 142 3)
1995	13.1	(0.0, 31.1)	444.0	(339.5, 603.3)	149.6	(106.3, 192.9)	10.5	(3.8, 17 2)	13.1	(0.0, 28 0)
1996	20.4	(0.0, 42.0)	544.3	(422.5, 716.9)	334.2	(185.8, 482.6)	32.1	(18.8, 45.4)	50.4	(0.0, 105.5)
1997	35.1	(0.0, 72.7)	481.4	(375.2, 633.9)	256.3	(197.7, 314.9)	11.5	(4.1, 18 9)	38.8	(13.9, 63.7)
1998	4.0	(0.0, 8.1)	429.4	(333.3, 563.5)	243.1	(132.4, 353.8)	11.4	(6.7, 16.1)	67.1	(0.0, 145 3)
1999	15.9	(0.0, 33.3)	493.4	(385.7, 648.7)	219.6	(170.8, 268.4)	11.6	(7.5, 15.7)	26.0	(9.1, 42 9)
2000	34.7	(12.9, 56.5)	529.7	(411.4, 699.6)	325.2	(240.3, 410.1)	11.9	(6.2, 17.6)	65.3	(0.0, 142.5)
2001	22.8	(0.0, 47.9)	488.7	(382.9, 648.5)	303.6	(232.3, 374.9)	23.4	(15.0, 31.8)	94.5	(1.2, 187.8)
2002	33.7	(6.5, 60.9)	492.7	(384.2, 659.0)	247.4	(191.1, 303.7)	46.0	(30.5, 61.5)	65.8	(0.0, 140.1)
2003	16.2	(6.2, 26.2)	502.5	(391.6, 661.7)	317.5	(223.2, 411.8)	14.7	(8.2, 21 2)	124.3	(0.0, 315 8)
2004	17.7	(5.9, 29.5)	548.0	(426.9, 738.1)	396.2	(271.5, 520.9)	8.4	(3.9, 12 9)	286.0	(0.0, 618.6)
2005	13.7	(4.3, 23.1)	509.1	(401.7, 667.8)	320.4	(233.4, 407.4)	23.2	(13.2, 33.2)	95.9	(5.7, 186.1)
2006	72.5	(30.8, 114.2)	521.9	(406.3, 689.7)	245.5	(195.5, 295.5)	9.7	(4.6, 14 8)	65.3	(0.0, 137.4)

[a] Estimates for mallards, American black ducks, green-winged teal, and ring-necked duck from Bayesian hierarchical analysis using FWS and CWS data from strata 51, 52, 63, 64, 66-68, 70-72. All others were computed as harmonic means of FWS and CWS estimates for strata 51, 52, 63, 64, 66-68,70-72.

[b] Common, red-breasted, and hooded.

[c] Greater and lesser.

[d] Common and Barrow's.

[e] Black and surf.

Appendix I. Abundance indices (in thousands) for North American Canada goose populations, 1969-2006.

Year	North Atlantic[a,b]	Atlantic[a,b]	Atlantic Flyway Resident[a]	Southern James Bay[a]	Miss. Valley[a]	Miss. Flyway Giant[a]	Eastern Prairie[a]	W. Prairie & Great Plains[c]	Tall Grass Prairie[c,g]	Short Grass Prairie[d]	Hi-line[d]	Rocky Mountain[a]	Dusky[d]	Cackling[e]	Aleutian[h]
	Canada goose population														
1969/70										151.2	44.2		22.5		
1970/71									131.1	148.5	40.5	43.9	19.8		
1971/72							124.7		159.6	160.9	31.4	30.5	17.9		
1972/73							137.6		147.2	259.4	35.6	34.4	15.8		
1973/74							119.9		158.5	153.6	24.5	38.3	18.6		
1974/75							144.4		125.6	123.7	41.2	38.1	26.5		0.8
1975/76							216.5		201.5	242.5	55.6	25.4	23.0		0.9
1976/77							163.8		167.9	210.0	67.6	25.2	24.1		1.3
1977/78							179.7		211.3	134.0	65.1	37.1	24.0		1.5
1978/79							99.4		180.5	163.7	33.8	52.9	25.5	64.1	1.6
1979/80									155.2	213.0	67.3	31.0	22.0	127.4	1.7
1980/81							125.5		244.9	168.2	94.4	53.9	23.0	87.1	2.0
1981/82							131.8	175.0	268.6	156.0	81.9	58.7	17.7	54.1	2.7
1982/83							155.1	242.0	165.5	173.2	75.9	41.5	17.0	26.2	3.5
1983/84							135.6	150.0	260.7	143.5	39.5	40.8	10.1	25.8	3.8
1984/85							158.4	230.0	197.3	179.1	76.4	43.2	7.5	32.1	4.2
1985/86							194.8	115.0	189.4	181.0	69.8	61.3	12.2	51.4	4.3
1986/87							203.2	324.0	159.0	190.9	98.1	60.7		54.8	5.0
1987/88		118.0					209.2	272.1	306.1	139.1	66.8	96.8	12.2	69.9	5.4
1988/89					380.0		210.2	330.3	213.0	284.8	100.1	86.6	11.8	76.8	5.8
1989/90				82.4	494.0		231.8	271.0	146.5	378.1	105.9	81.7	11.7	110.2	6.3
1990/91				108.1	237.0		211.8	390.0	305.1	508.5	116.6	76.9		104.6	7.0
1991/92				91.6	414.2		202.5	341.9	276.3	620.2	140.5	93.3	18.0	149.3	7.7
1992/93		91.3		77.3	402.4	810.9	157.5	318.0	235.3	328.2	118.5	106.4	16.7	164.3	11.7
1993/94		40.1		95.7	390.0	1002.9	210.8	272.5	224.2	434.1	164.3	129.5	11.0	152.5	15.7
1994/95		29.3		94.0	375.3	1030.6	204.6	352.5	245.0	697.8	174.4	139.9	8.5	161.4	19.2
1995/96	99.6	46.1		123.0	350.5	1132.4	190.4	403.3	264.0	561.2	167.5	137.3		134.6	24.6
1996/97	64.4	63.2		95.1	414.7	1038.7	199.3	453.4	262.9	460.7	148.5	95.7	11.2[h]	205.1	24.0
1997/98	53.9	42.2		117.1	297.5	1212.7	125.9	482.3	331.8	440.6	191.0	137.7	21.3[h]	148.6	29.0
1998/99	96.8	77.5		136.6	454.0	1234.1	206.7	467.2	548.2	403.2	119.5	156.2	13.8[h]	169.6	28.6
1999/00	58.0	93.2		89.1	345.0	1497.4	275.1	594.7	295.7	200.0	270.7	172.9	15.5[h]	175.0	33.5
2000/01	57.8	146.7		102.7	329.0	1371.3	215.4	682.7	149.1	164.1	252.9	168.9	17.3[h]	176.2	29.8
2001/02	62.0	164.8		76.3	286.5	1612.3	216.3	710.3	504.7	160.9	217.1	141.8	17.2[h]	127.9	36.8
2002/03	60.8	156.9	1126.7	106.5	360.1	1635.0	229.2	561.0	611.9	156.7	205.9	140.4	16.7[h]	165.2	62.4
2003/04	67.8	174.8	1048.7	101.0	276.3	1600.7	290.7	622.1	458.7	203.6	215.6	159.2	14.9[h]	130.2	69.9
2004/05	51.3	162.4	1167.1	46.3	344.9	1583.1	254.7	415.1	400.8	177.2	207.4	173.3	21.8[h]	156.9	63.8
2005/06	49.2	160.2	1149.1	160.4	384.4	1686.3	185.4	444.4	499.8	234.7	247.3	140.6	11.9[h]	169.3	N/A

[a] Surveys conducted in spring.
[b] Number of breeding pairs.
[c] Surveys conducted in December until 1998; in 1999 a January survey replaced the December count.
[d] Surveys conducted in January.
[e] Surveys conducted in fall through 1998; from 1999 to present a fall index is predicted from breeding ground surveys (total indicated pairs).
[f] Survey incomplete.
[g] Only Tall Grass Prairie Population geese counted in Central Flyway range are included.
[h] Indirect or preliminary estimate.

Appendix J. Abundance indices (in thousands) for light goose, greater white-fronted goose, brant, emperor goose, and tundra swan populations during 1969-2006.

| Year | Light geese | | | | White-fronted geese | | Brant | | | Emperor geese[a] | Tundra swans | |
	Greater snow geese[a]	Mid-continent[b]	Western Central Flyway[c]	Western Arctic & Wrangel[d]	Mid-continent[d]	Pacific[e]	Atlantic[c]	Pacific[c,f]	Western high Arctic[c]		Western[c]	Eastern[c]
1969/70	89.6	777.0	6.9					136.6	5.1		31.0	55.0
1970/71	123.3	1070.2	11.1				151.0	141.1	8.1		98.8	58.2
1971/72	134.8	1313.4	13.0				73.2	121.8	3.0		82.8	62.8
1972/73	143.0	1025.3	11.6				40.8	122.4	2.7		33.9	57.1
1973/74	165.0	1189.8	16.2				87.7	128.0	2.7		69.7	64.2
1974/75	153.8	1096.6	26.4				88.4	119.7	3.7		54.3	66.6
1975/76	165.6	1562.4	23.2				127.0	117.1	5.0		51.4	78.6
1976/77	160.0	1150.3	33.6				73.6	136.1	10.9		47.3	76.2
1977/78	192.6	1966.4	31.1				42.8	151.5	11.4		45.6	70.2
1978/79	170.1	1285.7	28.2			73.1	43.5	126.2	3.2		53.5	78.6
1979/80	180.0	1398.1	30.5	528.1		93.5	69.2	141.3	5.1		65.2	60.4
1980/81	170.8	1406.7	37.6	204.2		116.5	97.0	186.1	8.1	93.3	83.6	92.8
1981/82	163.0	1794.1	50.0	759.9		91.7	104.5	117.1	4.0	100.6	91.3	72.9
1982/83	185.0	1755.4	76.1	354.1		112.9	123.5	107.2	2.1	79.2	67.3	86.5
1983/84	225.4	1494.5	60.1	547.6		100.2	127.3	128.4	5.1	71.2	61.9	81.1
1984/85	260.0	1973.0	63.0	466.3		93.8	146.3	136.0	8.8	58.8	48.8	93.9
1985/86	303.5	1449.3	96.6	549.8		107.1	110.4	126.9	9.4	42.0	66.2	90.9
1986/87	255.0	1913.9	87.6	521.7		130.6	109.4	98.5	10.4	51.7	52.8	94.4
1987/88		1750.7	46.2	525.3		161.5	131.2	131.6	15.3	53.8	59.2	76.2
1988/89	363.2	1956.2	67.6	441.0		218.8	138.0	120.9	14.3	45.8	78.7	90.6
1989/90	368.3	1724.3	38.6	463.9		240.8	135.4	141.1	10.5	67.6	40.1	89.7
1990/91	352.6	2135.8	104.6	708.5		236.5	147.7	119.5	12.2	71.0	47.6	97.4
1991/92	448.1	2021.9	87.8	690.1		230.9	184.8	108.2	9.5	71.3	63.7	109.8
1992/93	498.4	1744.1	45.1	639.3	622.9	295.1	100.6	113.6	10.8	52.5	62.6[g]	76.6
1993/94	591.4	2200.8	84.9	569.2	676.3	324.8	157.2	118.8	11.2	57.3	79.4	84.5
1994/95	616.6	2725.1	146.4	478.2	727.3	277.5	148.2	116.8	16.9	51.2	52.9[g]	81.3
1995/96	669.1	2398.1	93.1	501.9	1129.4	344.1	105.9	122.0	4.9	80.3	98.1	79.0
1996/97	657.5	2850.9	127.2	366.3	742.5	319.0	129.1	151.9	6.0	57.1	122.5	86.1
1997/98	836.6	2977.2	103.5	416.4	622.2	413.1	138.0	132.1	6.3	39.7	70.5	96.6
1998/99	803.4	2575.7	236.4	354.3	1058.3	393.4	171.6	120.0	9.2	54.6	119.8	109.0
1999/00	813.9	2397.3	137.5	579.0	963.1	352.7	157.2	127.1	7.9	62.6	89.6	103.1
2000/01	837.4	2341.3	105.8	656.8	1067.6	438.9	145.3	119.9	4.9	84.4	87.3	98.2
2001/02	639.3	2696.1	99.9	448.1	712.3	359.7	181.6	127.8	9.0	58.7	58.7	103.8
2002/03	678.0	2435.0	105.9	596.9	637.2	422.0	164.5	101.7	4.9	71.2	102.7	108.2
2003/04	957.6	2159.1[g]	135.4	587.8	528.2	374.9	129.6	111.5	7.7	47.4	83.0	95.0
2004/05	814.6	2344.2	143.0	750.3	644.3	443.9	123.2	101.4	10.0	54.0	92.1	68.7
2005/06	1016.9	2221.7	140.6	710.7	522.8	509.3	146.6	133.9	9.5	76.0	106.9	70.5

[a] Surveys conducted in spring.
[b] Surveys conducted in December until 1997/98; surveys since 1998/99 were conducted in January.
[c] Surveys conducted in January.
[d] Surveys conducted in autumn.
[e] Surveys conducted in fall through 1998; from 1999 to present a fall index is predicted from breeding ground surveys (total indicated birds).
[f] Totals exclude Western High Arctic brant. Beginning in 1986, counts of Pacific brant in Alaska were included with remainder of Flyway.
[g] Survey was incomplete